RELATIONSHOTS
A Practical Guide to Relationship Success

ERIC WOOTEN

Relationshots: A Practical Guide to Relationship Success. Copyright © by Eric Wooten.

All rights reserved. Printed in the United States of America.

No part of this book may be used or reproduced in any manner whatsoever without written permission except in the case of brief quotations embodied in critical articles and reviews. Scripture is taken from the NASB version of the Bible.

For information, address DW Creative Publishers,
4261 E. University Dr. #30-355; Prosper, TX 75078.

DW Creative Publishers books may be purchased for business, educational, religious, or sales promotional use. For information, please email connect@dwcreativepublishers.com.

To connect with the author, Eric Wooten, visit www.AltaredMarriage.com

To subscribe and listen to episodes of RelationShots, visit www.youtube.com/@RelationShots.

FIRST EDITION

Cover design by: 360 Design Marketing, LLC
Interior design by: 360 Design Marketing, LLC
Editing by: Altared Marriage

PRINT BOOK: ISBN 978-1-952605-28-4
EBOOK: ISBN 978-1-952605-29-1

Library of Congress Control Number: 2003020090

To my wife, Jill, who's had a front row seat to the highs and lows of my personal and relational journey.

To my children, who have watched me get my relationships right and wrong at times.

To my parents, who have modeled love and commitment well.

To my community, the Marriage Mafia, who have supported, challenged and experienced this marriage journey with me.

CONTENTS

Chapter 1: The Three Secrets of Successful Marriages ... 11

Chapter 2: Five Truths Nobody Told You About Marriage ... 17

Chapter 3: The #1 Mistake Couples Make in Conflict ... 23

Chapter 4: Two Tips to Increase Emotional Connection ... 27

Chapter 5: Understanding Your Attachment Style ... 31

Chapter 6: Boundaries in Relationship ... 35

Chapter 7: Five Things That Hinder Sex in a Relationship ... 39

Chapter 8: How to Grow Your Friendship in Marriage ... 43

Chapter 9: Why "Fairness" Doesn't Work in Relationships ... 47

Chapter 10: Two Things Every Relationship Needs ... 51

Chapter 11: What Does it Mean to "Love" Someone? ... 55

Chapter 12: Three Things Husbands Want From Their Wives ... 59

Chapter 13: Three Things Wives Want From Their Husbands ... 65

Chapter 14: Four Keys to Resolving Conflict ... 69

Chapter 15: Five Communication Killers in a Relationship ... 75

Chapter 16: Is Your Baggage Impacting Your Relationship? ... 81

Chapter 17: Three Things That Damage Trust in a Relationship ... 85

Chapter 18: Eight Reminders of What Marriage Really Is ... 89

Chapter 19: Managing Differences ... 93

Chapter 20: Three Levels of Boundaries ... 97

Chapter 21: Five Things Every Marriage Needs ... 101

Chapter 22: Three Questions to Emotionally Connect With Your Spouse ... 105

Chapter 23: Managing the Moment ... 109

Chapter 24: How to Compromise **113**

Chapter 25: Myths About Marriage - Part 1 .... **117**

Chapter 26: Myths About Marriage - Part 2 .... **123**

Chapter 27: Seven Triggers for Those With Avoidant Attachment Style **127**

Chapter 28: Seven Triggers for Those With Anxious Attachment Style **131**

Chapter 29: Sacrifice is a Bad Marriage Strategy **135**

Chapter 30: Should Married Couples Have Friends of the Opposite Sex? **139**

Chapter 31: The Three Sides of Conflict **143**

Chapter 32: Three Keys to Emotional Safety **147**

Chapter 33: Resolvable Issues and Perpetual Problems **151**

Chapter 34: Five Mistakes We Make When Listening **155**

Chapter 35: The Three Phases of Love **159**

Chapter 36: The #1 Key to Success in Marriage **165**

Chapter 37: The Importance of Validation **171**

Chapter 38: Three Connection Killers **175**

Chapter 39: The Business of Marriage **179**

Chapter 40: Five Reasons to Combine Your Finances **185**

Chapter 41: Five Reasons Couples Stop Sharing With Each Other **189**

Chapter 42: The Power of Appreciation **193**

Chapter 43: What's Acceptable Sexually in Marriage? **199**

Chapter 44: Five Steps to Repairing After Conflict **207**

Chapter 45: The Secret to Staying "In Love" **211**

Chapter 46: Forgiving for Real **215**

Chapter 47: Six Characteristics of Healthy Relationships **221**

Chapter 48: The #1 Relationship Killer **225**

Chapter 49: Tips for Handling Difficult Conversations **229**

Chapter 50: How to Rebuild Trust After Lying **233**

Chapter 51: How to Maintain Healthy Sex in Marriage **237**

Chapter 52: Successful Couples Do This One Thing **243**

Introduction

You likely know someone personally who is recently divorced, has given up on the idea that enjoyable marriages exist or is currently choosing to just exist in a relationship where they've lost hope that things could be different or get better. Having been married for almost three decades and having worked with thousands of couples, I have felt like giving up at times and I've been convinced that "this is as good as it gets" in difficult relationship seasons. So it is with personal experience and professional expertise that I can confidently tell you that I understand how people can feel overwhelmed, frustrated and hopeless about relationships. However, building a great relationship is actually quite simple. Not easy…but simple.

If you are not yet married but desire to have a healthy framework and practical skills that will lead to success in marriage, this book is for you!

If you are single and have become frustrated with all the game-playing, unrealistic expectations, impractical relational "principles" and ineffective dating strategies so many relationship "coaches" and "experts" are putting forth…this book is for you!

If you're married and struggling with the connection, communication, and cycles of conflict issues common for so many couples, this book is for you!

If your marriage is good but you know that great is still before you and you see value in being intentional in your relationship, this book is for you!

My philosophy on marriage is really basic. If you've ever had a garden, houseplant or yard that you needed to take care of, then what I'm about to say will make perfect sense. The way you ensure that your houseplant, backyard tomato plant, rose bush or Bermuda grass lawn grows and thrives is a two-part approach.

1. You FEED it: whatever is needed for growth, you provide it. Water, direct or indirect sunlight, and fertilizer are necessary for growth. You regularly give the plant the things it requires to be healthy and grow.

2. You WEED it: whatever threatens to restrict growth, you remove it. You may pull the weeds. You may spray weed killer on the weeds. You may put chemicals in the soil to prevent weeds from growing up. If unattended, the weeds will grow with the plant and take some of the water and fertilizer intended for the plant which will prevent the plant from growing and thriving the way it needs to.

You provide for your plant and you protect your plant. And when you do those two things on a regular basis, your plant will grow, thrive and become all that it was designed to be. The same approach is what builds strong marriages! Did I mention that my philosophy of marriage is really basic? **I believe that marriage is a lifelong process of feeding and weeding.**

You will need to discover the things that make you and your partner feel connected and cared for in the relationship, and then feed your relationship those things on a regular basis. You will also need to uncover what things cause you each to feel disconnected in the relationship and then weed your relationship of those things on a regular basis, seeking to eliminate or minimize their presence. **Just like a houseplant, you will need to provide for and protect your relationship if you want to build a relationship that thrives and goes the distance.**

That's it. Pretty simple, right? Unfortunately, this isn't always easy because we are emotional, selfish, fearful and complicated people who tend to make relationships complicated, confusing, painful and combative. But I believe with everything in me that if you and your partner can be intentional about making sure that you are feeding your relationship the right things and weeding your relationship of the wrong things, you will have the kind of relationship you always dreamed was possible. As we begin this journey, I invite you to step into my living room, counseling office, couples retreat on a beach in Mexico or wherever you feel most at home and at ease, so I can share with you 52 ideas, thoughts and principles on relationships that are simple enough to understand and practical enough to apply.

HOW TO USE THIS BOOK

If you haven't figured it out by now, I'm pretty simple. This book has 52 chapters, one for each week of the year. If you love challenges, check lists and accomplishments, then by all means read one chapter each week with your partner and use the discussion questions at the end of the chapter to talk, evaluate and develop some practical actions that will either feed or weed your relationship.

If you want to take it slower and really focus in on one area for a longer period of time, then I would suggest reading one chapter per month. You can read the chapter together with your partner on the first day of the month, discuss the questions, and identify the actions you will take to practically apply the concept. Then set up a time each week to quickly (5-10 minutes) evaluate how you both are doing on implementing what you agreed to do. If the chapter was on the importance of validation and you decided to both work on validating each other's emotions when an issue was brought up, you would ask each other, "How do you feel I did this week in validating you?" You can evaluate once a week for the entire month to really make sure you are building this new habit into your relationship, before starting a new chapter the next month.

You can move through the book in order from one to fifty-two or you can look in the table of contents and pick and choose the topics that are of most interest to you. The key will be intentionality. If you want to see change in your relationship you need to be intentional. If you want to experience growth you will need to be consistent. Be honest with yourselves about how much time you will invest in your relationship, agree upon a plan, and get started. There is no right time, right way or right relationship. We all have the ability to create the kind of relationship we desire by consistently feeding and weeding.

If you want to add to your RelationShots experience you will find many of the same principles shared in this book in video form on my Youtube channel, Relationshots. You can read the chapter, head over to Youtube and search the topic on my channel, watch the video, and then come back and answer the discussion questions.

I am honored to join you on your relationship journey and I believe in you. Let's do this!

CHAPTER 1

THE THREE SECRETS OF SUCCESSFUL MARRIAGES

Whether this is the first relationship book you've ever picked up or just one of many on your bookshelf, I'm pretty confident that you've heard lots of "secrets," "keys" or "principles" over the years claiming to ensure marital success. You have read the introduction (or at least you need to) so you know that my philosophy of marriage is real simple. It's a lifelong process of intentionally feeding and weeding your relationship so that you ensure it continues to grow and thrive.

I have been married for almost three decades now and that philosophy of marriage still rings true. Different seasons of the relationship and life require that we feed the relationship different types of things and remove different types of weeds but the feeding and weeding never stop. As I said in the introduction, I have worked with thousands of couples over the past fifteen years and this philosophy of marriage still remains relevant. The areas of focus just change in different seasons. In one season you may need to be really intentional about times together of fun and connection because your schedules, jobs, raising kids and dealing with in-laws seem to take over the relationship, leaving little time for good relational connection together. In other seasons, you may be focused on breaking unhealthy conflict patterns that you have discovered are preventing you from resolving issues.

No matter the season, no matter the present issues, no matter the primary area of focus, I believe there are three foundational principles upon which every relationship must stand. These three areas are what I believe need to be consistently evaluated if you want a thriving marriage that is built to go the distance. Just about everything I talk about with couples in classes, online courses, weekend retreats and counseling sessions will fall into one of these three categories. The Three Secrets of Successful Marriages are Intentionality, Personal Responsibility and Community.

INTENTIONALITY

One of the myths that is destroying countless couples is the one presented in every romantic movie, romance novel and quite frankly even what many of us experience in the dating process. *It's the myth that in good relationships all the important relational stuff happens organically and spontaneously.* We're so in love that we naturally make time for each other, are attentive to each other's needs, prioritize each other, are naturally affectionate, positive, encouraging and communicate with ease. We just "get each other."

I'm not saying that doesn't happen in the dating process because it often does. Dating can be intoxicating because we are learning so much about each other and we are having so many new experiences together. There is probably no better feeling than when another person seems genuinely interested in learning about you and knowing you. That's dating. The problem is when our experience in dating creates a belief about marriage that things will stay the same. Communication, affection, conflict resolution, romance and sexual intimacy will continue to work out spontaneously because we're in love. Then when that's not the case, couples come to the conclusion that something is wrong with the relationship and they have "fallen out of love."

Don't miss what I'm about to say. This whole book and everything I believe about relationships stands on this truth: **Healthy marriages are Intentional marriages.** It takes time to learn each other and teach each other how you want to be cared for and supported in your relationship. Once you have determined what things are most important for you and your partner to feel connected, cared for, supported and protected in the relationship...your goal is to become highly intentional in these areas. It's not chemistry that keeps a relationship going, it's intentionality!

Communication, emotional intimacy, spiritual connection, fun together, sexual intimacy; whatever it is that you both have determined are key to your relationship, you become intentional about making sure you are doing these things consistently. You prioritize them. You plan for them. You schedule them and put them on the calendar. You don't leave the important things up to chance. You don't just do them when you are "feeling like it." Intentional marriages are successful marriages.

PERSONAL RESPONSIBILITY

In marriage we have both a relational responsibility (all the things I just mentioned being intentional about) and a personal responsibility to our spouse. Our personal responsibility is for our mental health, our emotional well-being, our physical health, our healing from past wounds and childhood issues, the development of good habits and behaviors and our personal growth. My wife and I made a marriage commitment to each other in our early 20's and we made that commitment to the person who stood in front of us. We didn't make a commitment hinging on some hope the other person would change all kinds of stuff. That's not a wise approach to marriage. But I can also say that neither of us almost thirty years later would want the twenty-year-old us with no growth, healing or maturity to be present in our fifties.

Many of the times I see couples divorcing and giving up on their marriages, it is not due to some relational issue. Their focus may be on the relational challenges they are struggling to resolve but the reality is that their struggles are driven by personal issues. One or both of them were unwilling or unable to overcome and heal from past personal wounds that were preventing them from relating in the marriage in a healthy way. Childhood wounds, past relational trauma, addictive behaviors and personal issues were creating toxic and dysfunctional behaviors in the marriage that were hurting the other person and damaging the relationship.

Both individuals in a marriage must be willing to take personal responsibility for their issues and be active in pursuing growth and healing personally so they can approach their partner from a healthy place. This is rarely a one-time endeavor but usually an ongoing process as seasons of life and relationship reveal individual areas that need attention and work. Sometimes couples even need to push the pause button on relational work in the marriage in order to focus energy individually on themselves, before coming back to addressing their relational struggles.

COMMUNITY

As you'll learn throughout this book, I'm a "community guy." If someone forced me to choose the one thing I believe to be most important for marriage, I'm going to go with community every single time. It's why I do marriage classes in groups. It's why I do marriage retreats with 6-10 couples. It's why I pour lots of my energy into our Marriage Membership Community. I'll dig into the concept of community in greater depth in Chapter thirty-six (#1 Key to Success in Marriage), but for now let me just set the table. Couples who are isolated are couples who are at greater risk of failing in their relationships than those who have good community around them. And when I say community, I mean other couples who are intentional about their marriages and are willing to be transparent and authentic with each other about the struggles of marriage. If you have a group of couples that you do fun stuff with, travel with and go out to eat with but don't actually share the real highs and lows of your relationship....that's camaraderie, not community!

Too many couples describe themselves as "private." They don't want others in their business. They don't want others to know where they struggle. They believe they are the only ones who are dealing with issues and have shame around the idea of others knowing what's going on in their relationship. So they stay stuck, depending on their own wisdom and strength to somehow get them out of their difficult place when they have already proven the inability to do so themselves.

Community provides some stuff we all need in marriage. Good community provides support, encouragement, accountability and a model of what marriage can be for us. You won't succeed in marriage if you are expecting your spouse to provide all these things for you. You'll hear much more about community throughout this book but know that I believe every couple needs authentic community to go the distance in marriage.

TAKE ACTION

Watch
The 3 Secrets to a Successful Marriage
on the Relationshots *YouTube* channel

1. On a scale of 1 to 5 rate your relationship on Intentionality. *(1 being not at all and 5 being very intentional)*

2. On a scale of 1 to 5 (1 being needs improvement and 5 being area of strength) rate yourself on Personal Responsibility.

3. On a scale of 1 to 5 rate your relationship on Community. *(1 being no community and 5 being good, authentic community)*

4. What is one area you each would like to be more intentional about?

5. What is one area of personal responsibility you need to grow in? What is one thing you will commit to do regularly to grow in that area?

6. What will you both commit to in the area of community? *(Find community if you don't have it; be more intentional with your community than you have been if you have it; etc.)*

Need community?
Check out the Altared Marriage Membership community.
www.altaredmarriage.com/membership

CHAPTER 2

FIVE TRUTHS NOBODY TOLD YOU ABOUT MARRIAGE

Alright, whether you're dating, newly married or have been married for 3 decades, it's time we get honest about marriage. The dating process sets us up for failure in marriage by teaching us the wrong skills needed for a successful marriage and then we send couples into marriage ill-prepared by not talking about what they are really signing up for. With wrong expectations in place, couples get blindsided by the realities of marriage and then assume something must be wrong and question the relationship. So let me give you 5 truths about marriage that you were likely never told, to both normalize what you are probably experiencing and help you adjust some unrealistic expectations that may have been causing unnecessary fear in your relationship.

Truth #1
MARRIAGE IS A COMMITMENT TO A SPECIFIC SET OF UNRESOLVABLE ISSUES

I know, pretty encouraging isn't it? The answer to the question that just popped into your head is YES! I am absolutely saying there are areas of your relationship that will never be resolved. We'll talk about this in more depth in Chapter 34, "Two Types of Conflict" but let me quickly explain. There are general issues that all couples deal with in marriage (communication, busy schedules, intimacy, conflict, etc) and there are specific issues that will be unique to you and whoever you chose to marry.

Some of these specific issues will never be resolved because it is part of who you are. Some of the categories that fall under this area of unresolvable issues are: personality temperament, basic needs, how you feel loved or cared for, organizational preferences, punctuality, need for closeness or independence and so on. You can make some small adjustments in these areas for each other but you won't fundamentally change how you are wired. The key becomes how you manage these differences. (Chapter 19)

Truth #2
MARRIAGE IS A FRONT ROW SEAT TO YOUR SPOUSE'S GROWTH PROCESS

If you've had an honest look in the mirror lately, you already know that nobody walks into marriage polished, perfect and fully mature. We all have some habits, attitudes and beliefs that need to be worked on or even eliminated. Hopefully, both you and your partner have done some work to grow, mature and to heal from past hurts before you entered the relationship. Whatever areas of your partner's life that still need growth, you will get a front row seat to this growth process.

The upside is that watching someone grow into who they were created to be is exciting and rewarding. The downside is that growth is not only painful for the individual growing but also painful for the person in relationship with them. If your partner has a greed issue that needs to be worked out in their life, that may happen at great financial loss to both of you. If you have a lust issue that has never been dealt with, that may negatively impact your partner in some areas of connection or intimacy. I could go on and on but you get the point. When the two become one, so do their issues and the growth that will be required to eliminate them.

Truth #3
MARRIAGE INVITES YOU TO BE A PART OF YOUR SPOUSE'S HEALING PROCESS

This one goes hand in hand with Truth #2. We all bring baggage into our relationships at varying levels and this baggage will impact the relationship.

Depending on the level of pain and trauma from your childhood and from past relationships and the work you have or have not done in healing and working through that pain, you will experience relational dynamics tied to those areas. This creates a frustrating yet rewarding situation where you are not able to do the work of your partner's personal healing but you will be a part of that healing process. You will either help their healing process or exacerbate the healing process based on how you respond to them, their triggers and their relational needs.

Relationships would be much easier if we stepped into it completely healthy and whole but that is never the case for anyone. Instead, we get the opportunity to help each other heal as we provide safety, security, compassion and care for one another. We don't get the option to say to our partner, "That issue happened before I knew you so it's not my problem."

Truth #4
MARRIAGE IS NOT MEANT TO BE FAIR

Many of the fights couples have in relationship are because they don't think things are fair. Fair is "good for good, bad for bad." Fair is "if you, then I." Fair is the expectation that whatever I am doing for you should be reciprocated in like amounts back to me. That's only "fair." The problem is that fairness isn't a good strategy for marriage and will only cause a couple to keep score and judge one another based on the evaluation of that score. Fairness is discussed in depth in Chapter 9 so I'll keep it brief here.

Lots of "good" people, "fair" people are getting divorced every day because they believed that marriage was supposed to be fair and they got tired of being the one who was giving more than they were getting. The problem with this fairness approach is that we give ourselves more credit for what we do and usually don't give the other enough credit for what they do. The right approach to relationship is to show up with a heart to give. If you are a person of faith, the Biblical approach to relationships is to give back better than you are given to.

Truth #5

MARRIAGE WILL TEST YOUR THEOLOGY

There are many well-meaning Christians who run into marriage where they see clear red flags, have real concerns about the other person or the relationship and just assume that "God will take care of it." They tell themselves that if both people are Christ-followers then "surely we'll be able to figure everything out because we've got God! He will give us the strength to handle whatever comes our way." I agree with that theological perspective but there is a huge assumption behind it that is usually not the case with many Christians. The assumption is the person is fully surrendered to God's will in every area of their life already and will be fully submitted to His will even when the relationship is painful, their needs aren't being met and they aren't happy in the marriage. The truth is that very few Christians exhibit this level of spiritual maturity to the point of complete selflessness and laying down their life, desires and happiness on behalf of another.

If you don't believe that marriage will test your theology then tell me you haven't heard a married Christian utter the words, "I know God hates divorce but...." That's a perfect example of a person's pain trumping their theology and instead of choosing to rest in God's grace to carry them through the difficulty of a painful marriage, they have decided to rest on God's mercy and forgiveness as they walk away from the marriage.

TAKE ACTION

Watch
5 Truths Nobody Told You About Marriage
on the Relationshots *YouTube* channel

1. Which of the 5 truths about marriage was most eye-opening for you and why?

2. Which of the 5 truths is the most difficult to accept for you and why?

3. What is one "unresolvable difference" you are aware of in your relationship?

4. What is one personal area of healing that either your partner has helped with in your life or that you would like them to help with?

5. What is one thing you need to do differently in your relationship with these 5 truths in mind?

CHAPTER 3
THE #1 MISTAKE COUPLES MAKE IN CONFLICT

Conflict isn't just possible in a relationship, it's inevitable. A relationship requires two people which means two different perspectives on just about everything you can think of. Conflict isn't even a bad thing, though many people avoid it like the plague. Conflict is the way a couple learns about each other, gains understanding of one another and ultimately grows closer to one another. The problem we have in relationship isn't conflict itself but how we handle and manage conflict when it arises. It becomes damaging rather than helpful to the relationship when we attack, criticize, minimize and hurt each other.

One of the mistakes I see many couples make when trying to manage and resolve conflict centers around a simple little phrase that I think most of us have likely said at some point in our lives. Remember, this is a "no judgment zone" and I'm your friend so be honest…show of hands if you have ever said the following to your partner in an attempt to get them to see your perspective…

"**How would you feel if I (fill in the blank)?**"
- How would you feel if I said that to you?
- How would you feel if I talked to another girl on Instagram like that?
- How would you feel if I had drinks with my boss at the company dinner?

- How would you feel if I didn't call you all day?

I know what you're thinking right now. What's wrong with that? It makes perfect sense. I'm trying to get them to see how their actions hurt me and how they wouldn't like it if I did the same to them. I get it. On the surface it makes sense but ultimately it doesn't actually do that and I'll give you two reasons I think "How would you feel if....?" should be eliminated from our relationships.

1. WE ALL HAVE DIFFERENT CAPACITIES

Every person has different emotional and relational capacities. What might be a big deal for one person, isn't for another. What makes one person feel insecure doesn't make another feel insecure. What feels disrespectful to one person does not feel disrespectful to another person. If you use the phrase, "How would you feel if..." in an attempt to get your partner to empathize with how you're feeling and the issue you present isn't a big deal to them, then your whole argument is now useless.

"How would you feel if I stayed out with my friends until 2am and never called or texted you when I was gone?" If your partner has no problem with that and responds with, "I'm fine with that," what do you say next? "How would you feel if I made a joke about you in front of everyone at dinner?" If your partner doesn't mind people making fun of them you have lost your leverage for trying to get them to understand how it hurt you.

It doesn't matter how they would feel if the same thing happened to them. What matters is how you felt. You simply need to share with your partner how you were hurt by their actions and that should be enough for them to care about how they impact you.

2. RELATIONSHIPS AREN'T ABOUT "TIT FOR TAT"

Relationships are supposed to be about mutual respect and care for one another. That means each partner should be considerate of the other in all things. The goal is not to require of the other person all the things they request of us just to keep things "fair." (see Chapter 9 for more on Fairness) If we operate with the "How would you feel...." mentality, we can then give ourselves a pass on doing things that are important to our partner on the basis that we don't need those things.

- I don't need affection from you so I'm not going to worry about giving you affection.
- I don't care about eating so I'm not going to cook for you.
- I don't ask you to put gas in my car so don't ask me to put gas in your car.
- I'll do my own laundry and you do yours.

The goal for relationship is not just reciprocity (e.g. What's good for you is good for me) but consideration (e.g. How do my actions impact you?) So, rather than using the "How would you feel...." approach to addressing issues, express a specific behavior or situation and how you feel about it. "I'm not comfortable with you talking to your ex-boyfriend as often as you do. It makes me feel insecure about us." "I worry about you when you are out all night and I don't hear from you. Would you be willing to shoot me a text once or twice during the night to let me know you're good?" Stop making this relationship mistake and be specific about how you feel and what you desire.

TAKE ACTION

Watch
#1 Mistake Couples Make in Conflict

on the Relationshots *YouTube* channel

1. What are some areas of your relationship that are a big deal to one of you but not the other?

2. Pick a couple of areas and explain to each other exactly why that particular behavior or situation is hurtful or difficult for you?

3. What adjustment or changes would you like your partner to do in this area?

4. What are some areas you have different capacities and shouldn't expect perfect reciprocation from your partner? (ie. parenting, energy levels, health, emotional/relational capacity, skill levels or aptitude?

CHAPTER 4

TWO TIPS TO INCREASE EMOTIONAL CONNECTION

It's not uncommon to feel disconnected in your relationship. In fact, I would say that emotional disconnection is guaranteed if you just choose not to be intentional. We all have a lot going on in our lives between work, kids, activities, friendships, travel and more. That's why even the best relationships will experience seasons where you both may not feel as emotionally connected as you would like but also can't figure out when to make time to reconnect.

Add to our busyness, the realization of how different men and women are when it comes to emotional communication and it can feel almost impossible to stay connected emotionally. I've found that many couples end up in a frustrating pattern where the wife is asking for her husband to connect with her and he's staring back at her wondering what that looks like. She gets frustrated that he doesn't just "know what to do" and he feels defeated not understanding what she really desires. This can just as easily be the other way around as well depending on each partner's connection needs and attachment styles; learn more about attachment styles in the next chapter.

Whether your disconnection is due to a lack of intention, the busyness of life or the differences between how you and your partner desire connection, with just a little bit of intentional effort you can begin to increase your emotional connection today. And don't worry if emotional conversations are not your thing. Here are two quick tips that anybody can use to increase emotional connection in your relationship.

#1: SHARE YOUR HIGH AND LOW FOR THE DAY

If you've ever asked your partner how their day was or how work was in an attempt to connect with them, only to be met with "fine, good or just like yesterday," this tip will help you dig deeper. If you really desire to connect on a more emotional level but don't what to say or how to do it, this tip will help you.

Sharing your high and low for the day does three things for your conversation. First, it removes the mystery of what to share and what not to share that keeps many couples from ever initiating a conversation. Second, it helps you both prepare for the conversation by paying attention to your day knowing what you will share. Third, it eliminates the possibility of feeling rejected by your partner. Sometimes people quit trying to initiate connection because the last time they did, their partner seemed disinterested in the conversation and they don't want to experience that feeling again. It may not have been disinterest but simply not knowing how to respond effectively.

Sharing your high and low for the day will allow you both to be prepared for what you will be talking about and will also give you access to each other's hearts and emotions as you are sharing at the "feelings" level. This will increase your emotional intimacy.

#2: USE COUPLES' QUESTION STARTERS

If you and your partner don't naturally dig below the surface level in your conversations, utilizing discussion questions can help. There may be a number of reasons you both stay at the surface level in your relationship that will require some deeper discussion or counseling to resolve. Things like lack of safety, fear of rejection, criticism, judgment and so on. If it's just because you don't really know what to talk about or how to go deeper, discussion questions will provide prompts and guidance for your times of communication together.

You can buy a book with couples' questions, purchase couples' card decks or just search the internet for couples' discussion questions and download a few. I would suggest you start by picking two nights during the week where you can commit to sitting down for 15-20 minutes together with no distractions. Put the phones away, turn off the tv and make sure the kids are in bed or busy so they aren't interrupting. Select two questions each and answer the questions. It's that simple. If you are enjoying your time and don't have anything else to get to, then keep it going. If you only have the agreed upon time, then just stick to the four questions and whatever conversation they stimulate.

Don't put too much pressure on these times together to produce some life-changing conversation. There may be times when you have really great conversations and there may be times it feels pretty mundane. The key is consistency. You are making the commitment to intentionally connect on a regular basis and this consistency will increase emotional connection. Just remember that the key is connection so avoid the following at all costs: criticism of the other person's answer, evaluating the other person's answer and giving correction or feedback on how the other person answered. Focus on listening and asking follow up questions to gain more understanding of your partner's perspective. This shows interest and care.

TAKE ACTION

Watch
2 Tips to Increase Emotional Connection in Marriage
on the Relationshots *YouTube* channel

1. Discuss with each other a couple of days and times that you will start prioritizing connection with each other and write down your commitment.

   Days: _____, _____

   Time: _____

2. Choose which approach you will use: high and low for the day or question cards. Try it for two weeks and then evaluate how you feel about it. Is it creating the connection you desire? If so, keep it up and add another day. If not, switch it up and try a different approach.

CHAPTER 5

UNDERSTANDING YOUR ATTACHMENT STYLE

If you're not familiar with attachment styles, let me give you a very brief overview of where the concept came from. Attachment theory originated with psychologist John Bowlby in the 1950's and was furthered by psychologist Mary Ainsworth in the 1970's. The focus of attachment theory is how people form relationships and bonds with each other. The basic idea is that we develop attachment styles based on how our early caregivers did or did not show up for us during childhood.

Why is this important? We often have unconscious beliefs and behaviors operating in our relationships that may be preventing or negatively impacting our ability to connect with our significant others. Understanding your attachment style and your partner's attachment style will be key in helping you both to better connect with each other in the relationship because attachment style impacts how a person deals with closeness and intimacy, how they respond to conflict and their ability to communicate emotions and needs.

I'll run through a quick description of the four attachment styles and then give you some thoughts on what to do with the information.

Secure Attachment: Those with a secure attachment style are easy to get close to, can depend on others and be depended upon and are not worried about rejection or abandonment. They are low on avoidance, low on anxiety and comfortable with closeness.

Avoidant Attachment: Those with avoidant attachment style value independence and freedom and often struggle with depending on others or having others overly dependent on them. They tend to be self-sufficient and may not want as much intimacy as their partner. They are high on avoidance, low on anxiety and uncomfortable with too much closeness.

Anxious Attachment: Those with anxious attachment often worry their partner will leave or abandon them and generally want more intimacy than their partners are often able to give. They tend to be insecure about the relationship and come across as needy. They are low on avoidance, high on anxiety and crave closeness and intimacy.

Disorganized Attachment: Those with a disorganized attachment (anxious-avoidant) are often uncomfortable with intimacy but also worry about their partner's commitment and love. They have traits of both the avoidant and anxious styles. They are high on avoidance and high on anxiety.

You may have recognized yourself in one of these four categories, and obviously if it was any other than secure, it's probably negatively impacting your relationship at times. If one of you is avoidant and the other is anxious then you already know the cycles you get stuck in where the anxious pushes for more closeness and reassurance only to be met with more distance and avoidance, triggering a greater push for closeness and receiving greater distance and avoidance. So, what do you do with the new knowledge and are you stuck with this attachment style for life?

The good news is that you can change your attachment style. The other good news is that you can begin doing some practical things to change faulty beliefs and implement behaviors that will value both partners' styles while seeking to increase connection. Here's what that looks like:

- Recognize your attachment style
- Recognize your partner's attachment style
- Identify when your style is triggered and communicate how you are feeling
- Practice asking for what you need that will help avoid triggers *(for more on triggers and attachment styles, check out Chapters 27 & 28)*

For instance, if you have more of an anxious attachment style and the disconnection or distance in the relationship is causing you to feel insecure and fearful, have a conversation with your partner. Let them know how you are feeling and that you desire some assurance from them that they are committed and care for you. This may be more frequent hugs, saying "I love you," or just prioritizing more intentional time together. If you have more of an avoidant style and feel a bit suffocated or overwhelmed by the amount of time together or expectations your partner has of you, then you can ask your partner for what you need. This may be a little more space or "me time" or just the opportunity to decompress after work before being expected to engage in emotional conversations.

The goal is for both partners to express empathy for how the other is feeling and find some small adjustments that can be made in the relationship to minimize or eliminate the triggers that are occurring. This will help you avoid negative cycles and keep you both connected in the ways you both desire.

TAKE ACTION

Watch
What's Your Attachment Style?
on the Relationshots *YouTube* channel

1. Identify which attachment style you most resonate with and why. Discuss with your partner.

2. Express some of the things that the other person does that trigger your fears or concerns in the relationship. (This is a time to listen and validate, not explain why that isn't your intention).

3. Share with each other some things you desire from the other person that would help you feel safer or more connected in the relationship.

4. Pick one of your partner's triggers to avoid and one of their desires to implement. Commit to these two actions for the next week and then revisit this conversation in a week and ask for feedback on how you did. *(Make adjustments and keep working to close the gap in your different relational desires).*

CHAPTER 6
BOUNDARIES IN RELATIONSHIP

Healthy relationships rise and fall on boundaries. In fact, I would say the quality of your relationship will be determined by the presence or absence of healthy boundaries. Dr. Henry Cloud, co-author of the book *Boundaries*, says the following about boundaries:

> "Boundaries define us. They define what is me and what is not me. A boundary shows me where I end and someone else begins, leading me to a sense of ownership. Knowing what I am to own and take responsibility for gives me freedom. Taking responsibility for my life opens up many different options. Boundaries help us keep the good in and the bad out. Setting boundaries inevitably involves taking responsibility for your choices. You are the one who makes them. You are the one who must live with their consequences."[1]

Many of the problems in relationships occur because someone is either not taking responsibility for their attitude or behavior or someone else is trying to take responsibility for something that isn't their responsibility. Boundaries solve these issues. You take responsibility for your emotions and actions, while not taking responsibility for your partner's emotions and actions. Neither of you requires the other person to take responsibility for what you should own.

---
1 Henry Cloud & John Townsend, Boundaries (Grand Rapids, MI: Zondervan, 1992), 31.

Sounds simple enough, doesn't it? The problem is that we don't always recognize our lack of ownership or responsibility because we may have grown up in a home where this wasn't practiced in a healthy way. So what seems normal and healthy to us might actually be enabling or avoiding ownership. Let's play a quick little game called "You might have boundary issues if...".

Score yourself one point for every statement that is true of you.

- You feel like people often take advantage of you for their own gain.
- You often have to "save" people close to you or fix their problems.
- You get more invested in a relationship than you should considering how long you've known the person.
- Your relationships tend to swing from great to horrible with not much in-between.
- You stay in break-up/make-up patterns too long in relationships.
- You spend a lot of time defending yourself for things you don't believe are your fault.
- You get sucked into pointless fighting or debating regularly.

If you scored higher on this game than you would have liked to, let's walk through some practical steps to setting boundaries in your relationships.

1. **Set a Boundary:** This is easier said than done. What will you tolerate or not tolerate in your life? What behaviors will you accept or not accept?
   Example. Your partner often criticizes you or yells at you....
   You decide that you are not going to put up with that type of behavior any longer and decide to set a boundary that will force them to own their anger and hostility towards you.
2. **Decide what the consequences are if someone breaks one of your boundaries.** This is bound to happen and often. It will be difficult to think of what the consequences should be once it does. You'll be biased by the person, the context and a myriad of other factors; so decide from the get-go.
   Example. When they yell at you or criticize you, that will be end of the conversation and you will...say goodbye and hang up if on the phone/

end and walk away from the conversation if in person...and will resume the conversation when they apologize and decide to talk respectfully to you.

3. **Communicate the boundary and consequence.** Make your boundaries known. Your partner must be clear on the boundary so they know when they are crossing the line.
Example. You tell them the behavior that you won't tolerate, how it impacts you and what you will do when they exhibit that behavior.

4. **Follow through.** If someone crosses your boundaries, do what you said you would. Be compassionate but be firm.
Example. The next time they cross this boundary you end the conversation respectfully.

A healthy relationship will require both partners to set boundaries and both partners to respect the other person's boundaries. If you have a hard time setting boundaries, then you need to address what your fears are in setting boundaries. Are you afraid your partner will be disappointed in you, get mad at you or leave you? If so, this needs to be addressed. If you have a hard time respecting boundaries then this needs to be addressed. Why do you struggle to respect their boundaries or why do you struggle to take ownership of your emotions and behaviors? Answering and navigating these questions may require the help of an outside mentor or counselor. If setting and respecting healthy boundaries in your relationship is an issue, don't hesitate to get some assistance. Boundaries are that important to your relationship.

TAKE ACTION

Watch
Boundaries in Marriage
on the Relationshots *YouTube* channel

1. Do you struggle to set healthy boundaries for yourself in this relationship or relationships with friends and family? If so, what is the fear in doing so?

2. Do you struggle to respect your partner's boundaries or other people's boundaries? If so, why do you think that is? Do boundaries feel like you're being controlled?

3. If you were to establish some boundaries with your partner that would make the relationship feel safer or more enjoyable, what would they be? Both partners share some *(maybe a spending boundary, language or tone used when communicating, rule around conflict, friendships, etc).*

4. Identify one boundary each and the specific consequence that will occur when it is crossed. Commit to keeping and honoring each other's boundary for the next week and then evaluate how you have both done after the week.

SOME EXAMPLES MIGHT BE:

- If you criticize or belittle me during an argument, I will end the argument and walk away. We can revisit the discussion once you have apologized.

- If you are unwilling to let me know when you will be home late for dinner, I will not prepare your food. You will have to take care of dinner yourself.

- If you choose to drink too much and come home late, you are not welcome to sleep in our bed. You will need to sleep on the couch that night since it interrupts my sleep and I don't like the smell of alcohol on you.

CHAPTER 7

FIVE THINGS THAT HINDER SEX IN RELATIONSHIP

I once heard someone say, "Sex is the easel upon which the relationship painted a picture of itself." To put it plainly, if the relationship is self-centered, the sex will reflect that. If the relationship is loving, the sex will be loving too. If the relationship is connected, sex will further the connection. If the relationship is disconnected, sex can become a routine, physical act.

You get the point! Sex is never "just sex." Sex is always relational which means the climate of the relationship in other areas will impact the sexual relationship. Some people use sex as a tool to connect because they don't know how to connect in emotionally or relationally. Some people use sex as a tool of reward and punishment to control and manipulate their spouse.

Sex is important and sex is powerful in a marriage. It has the ability to further connect a couple or the ability to cause division and resentment. Sexual intimacy also seems to be impacted by just about everything else in life and relationship. Emotions, stress, conflict, headaches, fatigue, body image issues, children, busyness, hygiene and whatever else you can fill in the blank with seem to impact a couple's sexual relationship. Because sexual intimacy is an important aspect of the marriage relationship, let's look at five things that can hinder sex in marriage.

1. GUILT

There are a lot of people who deal with guilt for things they have done in the past sexually, for relationships they've had, for the way they have used sex. These feelings of guilt don't just drift away because those actions or circumstances are ancient history. A lot of Christians who aspired to reserve sex for marriage and maintain their virginity, feel guilt for not doing so. Many individuals who vowed not to do something sexually or with somebody specifically but fell short of that goal feel guilt. Sex is then attached to that guilt and even though they are married and God is pro-sex for their marriage, they still struggle to separate their guilt from the current sexual relationship which was not the source of that guilt.

2. INADEQUACY

Pornography and romance novels can be blamed for a lot of why people feel inadequate in the bedroom. You start measuring yourself against what's going on in movies and pornographic images and you can start to believe that these performances are what the sexual relationship in marriage is supposed to be. Newsflash! They are actors, which means it's a performance, which means it isn't real! Yet I can't tell you the number of times I hear wives voice their frustrations that they feel like their husbands want them to be some high energy, seductive, role playing, gymnast-level flexible porn star in order for them to be satisfied. It's not just the wives; a lot of husbands feel like they aren't able to satisfy their wives. They feel like their wives are disappointed in them sexually and that they aren't measuring up to the expectations set in movies and romance novels. Nobody wants to feel like a failure, especially sexually, so feelings of inadequacy will cause spouses to avoid sex.

3. FEAR

Some of this goes along with inadequacy. If your spouse feels like they can't measure up to sexual expectations, they will be fearful of engaging sexually in order to avoid that possibility of failure. It could be fear of failure, fear of vulnerability, fear of rejection or fear of being judged for certain desires or fantasies. For some, fear of not knowing what to do because your spouse doesn't communicate about what they do and don't like will cause them to avoid sex.

4. SHAME

Now this is similar to guilt but much deeper. Guilt says, "I feel bad about what I've done." Shame says, "I feel bad about WHO I AM." There may be shame around childhood sexual abuse (something is wrong with me). There may be shame around sexual assault or rape (I'm damaged goods). There may be shame from what your spouse or past partners have said about the way you look, perform sexually or about your body. Shame will prevent people from being vulnerable and open, especially in the area of sex.

5. DISCONNECTION

A couple who is not connected emotionally and relationally will usually struggle to connect sexually. Now I know that the assumption is usually that women need to connect emotionally in order to desire connecting sexually but many men struggle in this area as well. I talk to men often who just don't desire their wives because of the constant criticism, judgment and verbal attacks they receive. When you don't feel emotionally connected in the relationship, sexual desire will usually diminish as well. Some people only know how to connect sexually and end up putting too much emphasis on this area of the relationship, ignoring or neglecting the need to connect emotionally, intellectually or spiritually as well.

These are only five of an infinite list of things that may be hindering healthy sexuality in your marriage. You'll evaluate these five areas specifically, but I encourage you to also discuss other things that personally may be hindering your desire or willingness to engage sexually in your marriage. Marriages that maintain a healthy and fulfilling sexual relationship are not those where everything just works spontaneously and organically but relationships where talking about sex is regular and intentional.

TAKE ACTION

Watch
5 Things That Hinder Sex in Marriage
on the Relationshots *YouTube* channel

1. Rate yourself on a scale of 1 to 5 on the five areas mentioned; guilt, inadequacy, fear, shame, and disconnection. *(1 being not an issue at all to 5 being a definite issue)*

2. What is one thing your spouse could do to help you in this area?

3. What is one change you would like to see in your sexual relationship *(frequency, activity, etc)*?

4. What is one thing you would like to see happen in your relationship outside of the bedroom that would help you to be more engaged in the bedroom?

CHAPTER 8

HOW TO GROW YOUR FRIENDSHIP IN MARRIAGE

Do you know that for all the differences between men and women, The majority of both men and women say that the **determining factor** in whether they feel satisfied with the sex, romance and passion in their marriage is **the quality of their friendship.** I don't know where the state of your friendship currently is with your spouse but if that high a percentage of both men and women say that friendship is important, I think it's worth a discussion. Some people would say your spouse should be your "best friend." I think that's great if they are but I also wouldn't say that has to be the case. It may be that you both have a lot of differences in what you enjoy doing, what you enjoy discussing and how you enjoy spending your free time and a "best friend" is probably someone that lines up with you in most or all of these areas. So, becoming best friends may or may not be realistic for your relationship. Your spouse should, however, be a really good friend and one of your closest friends for sure!

Since friendship is an important component of a good marriage and impacts satisfaction with sex, romance and passion, it's definitely worth strengthening. You already know my approach to marriage is consistent feeding and weeding; let's drop the category of strengthening your friendship under the feeding side of the equation. Yes, we need to focus on fixing issues in our relationships but let's take a few minutes to strengthen a great component of marriage, the friendship.

Friendship is simply a mutual respect for and enjoyment of each other's company. Couples who are good friends are well versed in each other's likes, dislikes, hopes, dreams and personality quirks! Show of hands...do you have a few personality quirks? I believe all marriages should consist of two people who are friends. I think everybody actually desires to be friends with their significant other but often don't know how to cultivate this or are unintentionally doing things to hurt the friendship. So, let's look at three characteristics of friendship so you can evaluate yourself in these areas and intentionally work on growing in these areas, which will strengthen your friendship with your partner.

A GOOD FRIEND IS SOMEONE WHO IS:
1. CONSISTENT

In relationship, one of the keys to your friendship is your consistency. We are all familiar with fair-weather friends or counterfeit friends...the ones who act like they are there for you but when times get tough, they scatter like cockroaches when the light comes on. We've all had friends that are all about us when it benefits them, when it gives them access to something they didn't have, when they are getting some kind of financial benefit but when they don't see any value being added in their direction, they disappear.

It's hard to maintain a close friendship with someone you don't feel like you can count on. It's hard to have a friendship with someone you don't feel "has your back." Ask yourself the following questions:

- Do you follow through on what you say you will do?
- Do you keep your promises?
- Is your support for your partner consistent or conditional?
- Can your partner count on you to be consistent in the areas of the relationship where they need you?

2. TRANSPARENT

Transparency does not just mean you don't lie, it's much deeper than that.

There are two components to transparency. First, your life is an open book to your partner. You don't have one life with them and another life on the side. You don't hide aspects of who you are or what you desire. Second, you speak truth to one another. Transparency requires you to speak difficult truths to each other because you love and care for one another. If you are fearful of speaking truth or you don't feel like taking the time and energy it requires to have difficult conversations, that's not being a friend. That is focusing on what is most comfortable for you. Privacy will erode friendship, while transparency strengthens friendship.

3. SYMPATHETIC

The root words making up sympathy simply mean "common passion." This speaks to the idea that friendship will arise between people who have common passions and interests. If you think about some of your best friendships in life, they probably started because you were interested in or involved in something you both enjoy. Maybe you played the same sport, were a part of the same club, joined the same fraternity or sorority or met at the 3-legged dog rescue mission or whatever it was. Friendship grows where there is a common interest or passion.

As you think about your relationship, what are some of the things that you both enjoy? Where is there already a common passion that you can connect around? What are some things you both would be interested in doing together? Don't overcomplicate it. Friendship grows as two spend time together doing things one or both really enjoy doing. It's a matter of intentionality and consistency and any two people can grow their friendship if they are willing to put in some time.

TAKE ACTION

Watch
How to Grow Your Friendship in Marriage
on the Relationshots *YouTube* channel

1. Rate yourself 1 to 5 in the areas of consistency, transparency and sympathy *(1 area of weakness and 5 area of strength)*. Then let your partner rate you since that's probably more accurate.

2. Ask your partner for one area where they would like you to be more consistent.

3. Ask your partner for one thing you could do that would make them feel you were being more transparent.

4. Identify one activity you both enjoy that you can commit to doing more consistently with each other.

5. Identify one new activity you both would be interested in trying together as you seek a new area of common passion.

CHAPTER 9

WHY "FAIRNESS" DOESN'T WORK IN RELATIONSHIPS

Hopefully you no longer yell things like "that's not fair" when things don't go your way but you likely think it at times in your marriage. Maybe you feel like you do more for your partner than they do for you. Or maybe you feel like you don't get the credit or appreciation for the things you do and the sacrifices you make. What I'm about to say might sound disappointing to you but trust me when I say this should release you from a lot of frustration and unrealistic expectations. You ready?

RELATIONSHIPS AREN'T FAIR!

There, I said it. Just rip that Band-Aid off. If your approach to a relationship is to expect or demand fairness, I'm here to tell you that's a bad strategy and approach. So let me define "fairness" and then tell you why I want you to release any expectation you may have for your relationship to be fair.

Fairness: in relationship it means that each person should receive to the same degree that they give. "I've been loving and giving towards my partner so they should be doing the same back to me. If they don't reciprocate, then I am justified in withholding my love for them." Our relational fears may convince us this is the right approach so we aren't taken advantage of and find ourselves in a one-way relationship but let me give you four reasons "fairness" doesn't work in relationships.

1. FAIRNESS LEADS TO PERFORMANCE

The foundation of a healthy relationship is attachment. Relationships are established on vulnerability, love and connection. When someone decides they aren't going to give more than they receive, the focus becomes performance. Fairness shifts the focus from connection to performance. Now they are in the relationship for what they can get and selfless love takes a back seat. Performance and fairness will leave you with no connection in the relationship.

2. FAIRNESS KILLS LOVE

Fairness is giving to get which has no place in love. Love is a gift we choose to give another person. I'm absolutely not saying that you just keep loving someone who is not caring for you back or mistreating you or abusing you, so don't hear that. I'm talking about our motivation in the relationship. Fairness will put you in a position to start keeping score and will never result in the love you truly desire from your partner. If you want to grow you need to practice grace, patience, sacrifice and serving. When you practice those things in your relationship the other person will feel valued and want to give the same kind of love back in a way that fairness never could.

3. FAIRNESS DISTORTS REALITY

The problem with living by the fairness ledger is that we are always more gracious to ourselves and more critical of our partner in our scoring. We tend to minimize the way we fail and maximize the way our partner fails. Even though we think we are operating by the "fairness" system we are unconsciously cheating and skewing the results in our favor. Operating in fairness will keep us convinced that we are being shortchanged.

If you're a person of faith, number four is for you!

4. FAIRNESS ISN'T GODLY

When you look at your relationship with God, aren't you glad He isn't fair? Fairness from God would mean you get to reap everything you sow. In fact, Psalm 103:10 says, "He has NOT dealt with us according to our sins, nor rewarded us according to our iniquities." If our goal is to "love our spouse the way God loves us," fairness can't be the standard we use to connect with each other.

Now, I realize the pushback you may be giving me in your head centers around the possibility the one person gives substantially more than the other for a long period of time. That definitely isn't healthy and ignoring that disparity in the name of avoiding a fairness mentality isn't what I'm proposing. If your relationship feels lopsided in the effort and care area, I would encourage you to:
- Communicate your needs
- Commit to giving whether you get or not
- When issues arise, address the specific issues rather than the "fairness"

Your relationship won't be healthy if one of you is doing all the giving, but it also won't be healthy if you're pursuing "fairness." Forget fairness and pursue love. Communicate your needs and ask for what you desire. Seek to serve each other in these ways without a focus on fairness.

TAKE ACTION

Watch
Why Fairness Doesn't Work in Relationships
on the Relationshots *YouTube* channel

1. Ask each other if you feel like there is a disparity in giving and serving in the relationship.
2. Has either of you developed some resentment in the relationship because you feel like you give more than the other? If so, share some specifics around this feeling.
3. What is one thing you desire more of from your partner that would help you to feel more cared for?
4. Express one action you are going to take based on this discussion to serve your partner or care for them in a more intentional way.

CHAPTER 10
TWO THINGS EVERY RELATIONSHIP NEEDS

Don't skip this one simply because I used the number two and you're thinking, "My relationship needs a lot more than just two things." Remember, we can only work on so many things at any given time so it's about focus, intentionality, mastery and then moving on to another area. I have found that many of our relational problems come from big swings to either end of a spectrum that has control on one end and independence on the other.

If you've ever found yourself in a relationship with someone who seems intent on controlling every aspect of the relationship and has an opinion on everything you do, you know how frustrating that can be. On the other hand, if you've ever had a relationship where the other person seems to give little or no thought as to how their actions impact you, that can be equally as difficult. I believe a proper understanding and application of a couple of key concepts can help navigate both situations. The two things every relationship needs are freedom and limits.

A lot of the power struggles that exist in relationships are between people who want to control too many things in the relationship and others who don't want their partner trying to influence or control anything they do. In some relationships, one person wants to do what they want, when they want and doesn't feel like they need to consider the other person with what they do.

In other relationships, one person wants to control everything their partner does and leaves little room for self-expression or independence. The answer to these power struggles and the key to a healthy relationship is found in a balance between freedom and limits.

Freedom and limits seem to be contradictory terms but they are actually quite complimentary when handled in a healthy, selfless way. Let's look at both and how they work together. As we do, let me also acknowledge that our attachment styles (Chapters 5, 27, 28) will impact how comfortable we are with both freedom and limits.

1. FREEDOM

Love only thrives in an atmosphere of freedom. If control and manipulation are regular occurrences, love in the relationship will die. If a person is unable to have an identity apart from their partner and the relationship, love will die. A healthy relationship requires two people to set each other free from control. Part of relationship is enjoying and valuing each other's differences and individuality, not thinking alike but thinking together. We shouldn't punish our partner for tastes that we wouldn't choose or for wanting time apart or for choices we don't agree with (assuming they are not immoral, unethical or illegal obviously).

If you truly love someone, you should be invested in them becoming the best version of themselves even if it has nothing to do with the relationship and doesn't benefit you. A healthy relationship serves not only the needs of the relationship but also the needs of each partner in the relationship. Freedom is necessary in a relationship but partners need to act responsibly with the freedom given them!

2. LIMITS

We all have the ability to get out of line without seeing it and we all can be blind to the things we do wrong at times. Then there are times we know we are wrong or out of line but we just don't care! In both of these situations we need limits placed on us by those with whom we have committed to be in relationship with. These limits are not based in selfishness for one partner, they are healthy limits that will allow the relationship to grow and thrive.

If you don't like the words discipline and correction, you will struggle in a healthy relationship. Two of the greatest gifts a good relationship can provide for us are correction and discipline! A healthy relationship isn't going to allow one partner's hurtful behavior to continue without confronting and challenging it. There will be times in every relationship when poor behaviors or attitudes are negatively impacting the relationship and there need to be limits put on these to keep them from taking over or severely damaging the relationship. Anger, addictions, abuse, selfishness, control, excessive criticism, etc., should not be allowed to continue unchecked in a relationship. A healthy relationship is one in which we express limits and let each other know when something wrong is happening.

Every relationship needs this combination of both freedom and limits for love to thrive. We give each other freedom but at the same time we choose not to take advantage of that freedom to pursue selfishness in ways that will hurt the other person or the relationship. We avoid trying to control each other but at the same time give each other permission to challenge behavior and set limits when we are behaving in ways that don't line up with the agreed upon values and virtues of the relationship. Freedom and limits work together in establishing a healthy relationship.

TAKE ACTION

Watch
2 Things Every Relationship Needs
on the Relationshots *YouTube* channel

1. On a scale of 1 to 5 how would you rate the balance of freedom and limits in your relationship *(1 not balanced, 5 great balance)*?

2. Do you desire more closeness and togetherness in the relationship or more space and independence?

3. Do you have any fears associated with your partner having freedom and independence in the relationship? This could be due to attachment style, past relationship hurt, dishonesty, or unfaithfulness in the relationship.

4. What are some things your partner could do to help you feel more secure as they also maintain freedom?

5. Do you struggle with limits being placed on you? If so, why?

6. Discuss what you believe to be healthy limits/boundaries in a relationship.

7. Are there any limits you feel need to be present in your relationship that currently do not exist?

CHAPTER 11

WHAT DOES IT MEAN TO "LOVE" SOMEONE?

It sometimes feels like the word "love" has lost its meaning. Think about how often we use it or should I say over-use it? I love you so much. And I love tacos. And I love sleeping in. And I love a good steak. And I love going on vacation. Sadly, some people spend more time and effort on their tacos and steak than they do on the person they claim to "love" above all else. I happen to believe that love is more than a feeling, more than an experience, and more than a state of mind.

When most people say, "I love you," what they are really saying is, "I love the way you make me feel." They are in love with what they are receiving from the other person and how that person is making them feel about themselves. This definition of love is self-focused. Love is meant to be other-focused. Love is both an internal commitment and outward action focused on the good of the other person.

Let me present three marks of unselfish love so that you can evaluate how well you are truly "loving" your partner.

1. YOU FEEL AND CARE ABOUT THE EFFECTS OF YOUR BEHAVIOR ON YOUR PARTNER

Many people don't fully grasp or care about how their behavior impacts their partner in relationship, but true love is a commitment to considering how your attitudes, habits and behaviors will impact another. This doesn't just apply to the big, obvious aspects of relationship like infidelity, dishonesty, and substance abuse. This also applies to the little things.

I feel like this is a safe space, so let me try some self-disclosure and vulnerability. I'm a procrastinator. When I was single, it didn't really matter that I would pull all-nighters before an exam because I didn't study ahead of time. It didn't impact anyone else when I showed up at the airport with barely enough time to get through security and still make my flight. When I decided to get married, however, loving my wife meant I needed to consider how my behavior in these two areas would impact her. Last minute behavior on my part only adds stress and unnecessary anxiety in my wife's life, so "loving" her means I don't put things off and arrive a bit earlier.

2. YOU THINK FIRST OF MAKING YOUR PARTNER'S LIFE BETTER

Loving your partner means you learn what makes them feel cared for and valued and regularly look for opportunities to do those things for them. You ask about their hopes and dreams and look for ways to help them achieve those goals. You put yourself in their shoes and imagine what it would be like to be them. That means you don't come home from a hard day's work, walk in the door, and find a place to unwind without checking in with your spouse to see how their day was and what they may need from you. It means you don't make decisions only focused on how they will impact you. Selfish love says, "What can they do to make my life better?" Selfless love says, "What can I do to make their life better?"

3. YOU WANT THE BEST FOR YOUR PARTNER EVEN WHEN THEY CAN'T SEE IT

I might step on your toes a bit here, so repeat this after me. "Eric, you are my friend." Okay, now that we've settled that...love means you don't avoid the tough conversations because it might cause you discomfort. Love may require difficult confrontation or intervention. If your partner has a substance addiction you may need to intervene at some point. If they continue to exhibit unhealthy behaviors in the relationship, it may require difficult boundaries to force them to take responsibility for their actions. If they create an environment in the relationship that is unsafe, it may require separation.

In some situations, loving your partner may be tough because it requires your willingness to risk the current atmosphere of the relationship or even the future of the relationship in order to put their "best" first. This will be especially true in the moments when they don't feel like this is for their best or they don't like being held accountable for their actions. If you are unwilling to have tough conversations or set healthy boundaries in your relationship out of fear of retaliation or withdrawal, that is a sure sign that you love your comfort or the relationship more than you do the other person and their best.

TAKE ACTION

Watch
What Does It Mean to Love Someone?
on the Relationshots *YouTube* channel

1. Rate yourself on a scale of 1 to 5 on the 3 marks of unselfish love. Give some specific examples of why you gave yourself that score *(1 being needs improvement and 5 being area of strength).*

2. Ask your partner if there are any areas of your behavior where they feel like you don't fully grasp how it impacts them.

3. What are some ways you think first about your partner's best over what you desire?

4. Are you comfortable having hard conversations or confronting your partner's behaviors? If not, why?

5. What is one thing you can do this week to show selfless love to your partner?

CHAPTER 12
THREE THINGS HUSBANDS WANT FROM THEIR WIVES

All right, let's get this out of the way first. Too often we feed the narrative that all men really want from their wives is sex. And wives, you may be nodding your head thinking, "That's pretty much the case in this house." Sex is definitely a high priority for a lot of men but I want to propose the idea that if they were getting some of the other things high on their list of needs, what appears to be a narrowly focused desire for sex may not seem as great. What are those other things, you may be asking? Now that we've addressed sex, let's look at three things (not named sex) that husbands desire from their wives.

1. ENCOURAGEMENT

Men aren't always the most communicative about their emotions and feelings, so you don't always know when they are down, discouraged or overwhelmed. Boys don't grow up in environments where they are rewarded for sharing their emotions. I don't remember a single time growing up where I was encouraged to just "be sad," "let it out," or "have a good cry." And my father is a counselor so we definitely had a more emotionally expressive environment than the one in which a lot of people are raised.

Understanding and expressing emotions is likely not a skill that your husband has practiced with regularity. He may never tell you the emotional weight he is carrying. He may never share that he is discouraged and feels like giving up at work or that he doesn't know what to do with the drama in his family. But I can guarantee you that your encouragement means everything to him.

ENCOURAGE YOUR HUSBAND... BE HIS CHEERLEADER... TELL HIM THAT YOU'RE FOR HIM AND BELIEVE IN HIM.

Ask if he needs your support and what support looks like to him. The world will beat him up so when he gets home be an encourager!

2. ADMIRATION

When surveyed, admiration consistently rises to the top of the list as one of men's most important emotional needs. Husbands want their wives to admire them. They want their wives to speak well of them to others. They want to be recognized for their strengths. They want to know that their wives are "into them" and feel fortunate to be with them.

Our tendency in marriage can be to highlight our spouse's weaknesses because those are usually the things causing us relational pain and so we want to see change. I'm not for a minute implying that wives can't ever point out an issue, address inconsistencies or challenge unhealthy behavior, but criticism is the exact opposite of admiration so wives must be intentional about spending more energy and time pointing out what they admire than what they dislike. Tell your husbands what you value about them, and do it often.

Most men feel an internal pressure to excel and are constantly comparing themselves to their peers for validation. Whether they verbalize it or not, men are evaluating themselves against other men based on salaries, accomplishments, physique and more. Make a regular habit of pointing out those things you admire about who they are.

3. APPRECIATION

You may be thinking that appreciation sounds just like admiration so let me distinguish between the two. Admiration is focused on who your husband is, affirming his value and worth. Appreciation focuses in on what he does. It's an acknowledgment of his efforts. If you've ever had the argument with your husband where you tell him you don't feel like he loves or cares about you and he responds by describing all the things he DOES FOR YOU and the family, you got a glimpse of his desire for appreciation.

Men are wired to do things, to provide, to "feed" the family. Now women need emotional connection and bonding more than they need to be "fed" but a husband's natural inclination is to provide for the family and so they do things. They work. They build. They fix. They mow. They play video games. Just kidding about the video games. That doesn't actually help anybody.

If men don't receive appreciation for the things they are working hard to do, it feels to them like their wives don't value them. There may be no worse feeling than when you are working hard to provide value and help only to be told "you don't do anything." Our natural inclination is to notice what's going wrong so you must be highly intentional to look for and appreciate what's going right, especially when it comes to chores, responsibilities or activities that are regular and expected. You won't often think to appreciate your husband for going to work, taking out the trash, getting the oil changed in the car or whatever other responsibilities they naturally take care of.

Wives, show some appreciation. Tell him how you appreciate something he has done. Tell him how grateful you are that he consistently _____. Tell him "thank you" when you see him do something for you or the family. Catch him doing something right and then express appreciation!

Husbands want their wives to encourage them, to admire who they are and to appreciate what they do. When men receive these things their emotional tanks will be full and their investment in and commitment to their marriage and family will strengthen. Many of the escapes men turn to are an attempt to avoid the discouragement and criticism they often feel at home. Encourage, admire and appreciate your husbands and watch their hearts open up.

TAKE ACTION

Watch
3 Things Husbands Want From Their Wives
on the Relationshots *YouTube* channel

1. Rate yourself on a scale of 1 to 5 on encouragement, admiration and appreciation *(1 being needs improvement and 5 being area of strength)*. Give some specific examples of why you gave yourself that score.

2. Ask your husband for some specific things you could do that would feel encouraging to him.

3. Ask your husband for some specific things you could do that would show admiration.

4. Ask your husband for some specific things you could do that would show you appreciate what he does.

5. Ask your husband for some specific examples of how he feels criticized and unappreciated.

6. Commit this week to creating an atmosphere where you are encouraging, admiring and appreciating your husband in at least a 3 to 1 ratio compared to criticism.

CHAPTER 13

THREE THINGS WIVES WANT FROM THEIR HUSBANDS

Men tend to avoid counseling, marriage classes and relationship retreats because, well, they can be a bit overwhelming. It can feel like an opportunity for their wives and counselor to team up against them, reminding and reprimanding them for everything they do wrong in the relationship. Because emotional and relational connection don't always come naturally for a lot of men, any type of relationship work can quickly become frustrating and exhausting. Men can feel like they are being asked to perform Olympic level gymnastics when they're barely comfortable with the cartwheel.

So men, I'm your friend and I'm here to help. Forget all the noise. Forget all the staring into your wife's eyes for thirty seconds while you connect emotionally. Forget softening your tone and using "I" statements. Let me simplify this relationship stuff by giving you three simple things your wife desperately desires from you.

1. BELIEVE IN HER

What you believe about your wife will influence who she becomes! Husbands, you have the power to bring about change, growth and the fulfillment of potential in your wife. No matter how beautiful your wife is, there's something she doesn't like about herself. No matter how confident she is, insecurities will haunt her at times. No matter how successful she is, at times she'll wonder if she measures up.

There's a whole world out there full of people ready to criticize, attack and condemn your wife, so they don't need more of that when they walk in the door at home. Many wives today have bought into the myth they should be able to simultaneously be an amazing wife, mom of the year, great friend and climb the corporate ladder. Wives naturally will question whether they're doing enough while comparing themselves to some unrealistic caricature being put forth on social media.

Husbands, listen to your wife, appreciate her and encourage her. Make sure she knows that even when everyone else doubts her, you believe in her!

2. UNDERSTAND HER

Don't close the book! Hold on a minute and let me explain. I get it, the thought of actually understanding a woman seems impossible and may be, so let me simplify this one a little. If you are a person of faith maybe you're familiar with the Bible verse that says, "Live with your wife in an understanding way." (1 Peter 3:7) You likely will never fully understand your wife because you are both wired in fundamentally different ways. You can, however, commit to being a lifelong learner of your spouse, seeking to understand how she thinks, what she needs and how she is different from you.

Understanding requires both asking questions and listening. Listening means you are not thinking about what you're going to say when she stops talking. Listening means you don't make judgment about what she is saying and how she is saying it. Listening means you are able to repeat what was said and identify what you think she is feeling. You won't be able to understand your wife if you aren't regularly talking with her, listening well and asking questions for greater understanding.

Your wife wants you to understand how she feels about the family, being a mother, her career, her parents and childhood, her concerns with you, her dreams, the losses she's experience in life, her stressors, her friendships and what she hopes to be doing ten years from now. Your wife wants you to "get her" and that requires understanding how she is experiencing the world and relationships around her.

3. ROMANCE HER

Now, every person is different and although stereotypes and generalizations are usually mostly true, I'm sure some of you husbands are thinking my wife isn't romantic or the wife is saying skip this one, I don't like romantic stuff. Let me define what I mean by "romance her."

In a national survey where women were asked what was the most important thing to them in a relationship, they said overwhelmingly that "we need to feel appreciated, wanted and loved." That's romance. It's not always some fantasy or surprise.

When women were asked for practical things that men could do that are important for romance, here were the top answers:

- He touches me with tenderness
- He treats me as the most important person in his life
- He snuggles after sex
- He is available when I need help
- He gives emotionally
- He shares his thoughts and dreams with me
- He arranges for us to have time alone

Notice only two of those had to do with touch, affection or sex, so for those of you who don't consider yourself or your wife romantic, it's not just flowers, bubble baths and spontaneous getaways. It's anything that communicates you are valuable, I'm grateful for you, you are special and you're important to me! These are the things that "romance" your wife, men.

TAKE ACTION

Watch
3 Things Wives Want From Their Husbands
on the Relationshots *YouTube* channel

1. Rate yourself on a scale of 1 to 5 in the areas of Belief, Understanding and Romance *(1 being needs improvement and 5 being area of strength)*. Give some specific examples of why you gave yourself that score.
2. Ask your wife for some specific things you could do that would cause her to feel you believe in her.
3. Ask your wife for some specific things you could do that would show you seek to understand her.
4. Ask your wife for some specific things you could do that would cause her to feel romanced.
5. Commit this week to implementing some of the specific actions your wife expressed she desires from you.

CHAPTER 14
FOUR KEYS TO RESOLVING CONFLICT

Conflict is an inevitable part of relationship because no two people are exactly the same and different perspectives will be present on a variety of issues. People have different backgrounds, sometimes different cultural perspectives, different experiences in life, different preferences and biologically, men's and women's brains are different in structure and internal chemistry.

Because differences will lead to conflict, it's important that couples learn how to come to an agreement with each other without running over each other. If not, conflicts will lead to fights rather than resolution and my guess is that you and your partner desire resolution.

Listen, there's nothing more frustrating than the experience of having conflict in your relationship without the ability to resolve it. That allows bitterness and resentment to creep in and if you try to resolve conflict unsuccessfully for too long, there will come a time when you give up altogether and just decide it's not even worth engaging anymore. Over the years, I've discovered that the key to resolving conflicts begins with our assumptions long before the conversation has ever started. It's not just what happens during the conflict that is important but also the assumptions and beliefs we bring with us into the conflict. Let me give you four keys to consider when it comes to conflict in your relationship according to psychologist Willard Harley. [2]

1. YOU MUST HOLD YOUR PARTNER'S PERSPECTIVE IN HIGH REGARD

It all begins here. If you don't generally hold your partner and their perspectives in life in high regard, I might ask you why you are with them? It could be that you value their thoughts in one area of life but not in others. If you are entering a conflict knowing that you don't hold their perspective in high regard, you are going to have a really hard time feeling any motivation to listen to or move towards their perspective. I encourage you to remember your partner is not the enemy and their perspective should be held in high regard. This is the starting point for a willingness to listen and seek understanding.

2. YOU MUST BELIEVE THAT YOU DON'T HAVE ALL THE ANSWERS

I'm hoping that you don't believe you have all the answers but a lack of self-awareness can creep up on all of us. The main reason for the current political divide in our country is the belief that "our side" has the answers, which can actually allow us to believe that those who don't see like us are not just wrong but stupid. How arrogant a belief it is to come to the conclusion that we are so right that those who don't see like us are blind, uninformed, evil or worse!

In relationship, if you believe you have all the answers or even most of the answers, you will not be open to any perspective that is in any way contradictory to yours. This will prevent you from compromising your position in order to arrive at mutual agreement. We have to at least be open to the possibility that our perspective could be flawed.

---

2 Willard Harley, He Wins She Wins (Grand Rapids, MI: Revell, 2013),22.

3. YOU MUST VALUE YOUR PARTNER'S POINT OF VIEW AS PART OF THE SOLUTION

Please notice I said, "As part of the solution." This means you can't get away with saying, "I hear and really value your perspective but I still think we need to do things entirely my way."

Conflict resolution is often like putting a puzzle together, taking pieces of what you both see and putting them together in such a way that both of your perspectives are essential to the final solution. A successful solution requires multiple perspectives. Your perspective is only one approach and a limited one at that.

4. YOU MUST UNDERSTAND THAT MUTUAL ENTHUSIASTIC AGREEMENT IS THE ONLY SOLUTION

This can often be counter to our tendency in relationship which is to give in, give our partner their way, keep the peace and move on. I cover "Why Sacrifice Is a Bad Marriage Strategy" in Chapter 29, so check that out for more on this topic.

The goal of resolving conflict in a relationship should be to find an enthusiastic mutual agreement. Yes, I did say enthusiastic. I don't mean you're high-fiving after the resolution has been found but that should be the posture of our heart. It's not enthusiastic because we got our way but enthusiastic because the combination of your collective minds has found a solution far better than your ability to do so individually!

Both of you should walk away feeling good about the agreement rather than one of you giving in and feeling resentment under the surface because you gave in once again just to keep the peace. That is not a successful long term strategy. It's the differences in perspectives that make you and your partner a good team. You need each other's brains and you need each other's perspectives. You are making a huge relational mistake if you begin to view your partner's different perspectives with contempt and condescension.

None of us will ever be smart enough to ignore or discount other people's perspectives in our lives. I'm guessing you picked your partner because you saw value in who they are. Keep that in high regard and seek mutual agreement in conflict.

TAKE ACTION

Watch
4 Keys to Resolving Conflict
on the Relationshots *YouTube* channel

1. Take two minutes and write down a few things you value about your partner. Now share those things with each other.

2. Give each other one specific example of a perspective or decision the other person has made that you think was wise.

3. Come up with one conflict where one of you felt like you just gave in to move on rather than reaching enthusiastic, mutual agreement. Share what solution would have made you feel better about the resolution.

4. Share with each other what you desire in future conflicts that would make you feel like your partner values your perspective and is seeking enthusiastic, mutual agreement.

CHAPTER 15

FIVE COMMUNICATION KILLERS IN A RELATIONSHIP

The number one presenting problem for couples that seek counseling is communication. The majority of couples that are having issues in their relationship attribute these issues on some level to their inability to communicate. The problem most have is that they only recognize the ways the other person is hurting their communication which is clearly only half the problem and the only thing they can't actually control. Don't get me wrong, I do believe relationships work best when both people are willing to address issues and make changes but you and I will never be able to control what the other person is or isn't willing to do. We can; however, change how we show up and communicate in the relationship.

Solving problems, discussing finances, parenting, resolving conflict or just deciding where to eat or dinner is difficult when you can't communicate with your significant other. While many communication issues are unique to each couple based on their upbringing, preferences and the emotional state of the relationship, there are also some universal communication principles that apply to every relationship. Let's look at five communication killers, that i present, will hinder your ability to communicate effectively with your partner.

1. MINIMIZING

If your partner feels strongly about something or thinks something is significant, whatever you do, do not minimize it! What does minimizing look like? "Oh, it's not that bad." "It doesn't hurt that bad." "That's not near as bad as _____." "I've had worse." Hearing any of those phrases will kill any hope the other person had that you may actually care about them and will seek to understand them.

Even if you don't feel like their issue is a big deal, that's not important at that moment. The issue is big to them and if you want continued access to their heart you have to connect with how they are feeling in the moment. Sometimes we minimize in an attempt to help them not stress so much or not hurt so much about the situation but that rarely helps them feel better. Instead, they walk away feeling like you don't understand or care about what they are dealing with. Focus on connection rather than solution and you'll avoid minimizing.

2. DEFENSIVENESS

Defensiveness is simply anything you do to fight off feeling bad. Expressing anger, attacking, pouting or whatever your defensive "go to" is probably won't help your communication improve. All defensiveness will do is shut your partner down. When you defend yourself, you simply communicate to the other person that you are closed and unwilling to hear anything about your behavior.

Justifications, excuses and explanations are all defensive tactics that communicate the other person's message isn't welcome and neither are they. Listen to your partner, take in the message, embrace the feedback and you'll communicate you are more willing to hear than defend. If you struggle with getting defensive or responding with "your truth" in the moment your partner brings an issue to you, check out Chapter 23 on "Managing the Moment" for tips on eliminating defensiveness.

3. SARCASM

We're friends and this is a safe place so let me just be vulnerable for a moment. Sarcasm is my biggest problem when it comes to communication. I've always got a joke or comeback on the tip of my tongue and since I'm a little bit passive-aggressive, sarcasm is the perfect weapon for me. I like to use sarcasm and jokes to cover how I really feel instead of honestly expressing myself. That way if the other person gets upset or offended I can just respond that I'm joking. Unfortunately, sarcasm communicates disdain and disrespect. Sarcasm hurts, closes hearts and takes conversations in the wrong direction.

4. UNIVERSAL STATEMENTS

If "always" and "never" show up in your conversations then you understand universal statements. These extreme statements don't communicate reality so you have already lost your message if you choose to use universal statements. Not only are these statements untrue but they leave the other person feeling judged and bad about themselves.

Universal statements actually move you farther away from what you are trying to communicate because people get stuck on the total failure you are communicating to them. If you say something like "You never show love to me," your partner will lose hope in the relationship as they recount the things they believe they do to express love and conclude that if those don't count for anything they might as well quit trying. Instead of using universal statements focus on what you are in need of and ask for those things specifically. "I would like you to be more affectionate with me." "I would like you to stop raising your voice when we aren't seeing eye to eye." "I would like you to put your dishes in the dishwasher so I don't have to."

5. SHUTDOWN STATEMENTS

Shutdown statements are the things you say when you are hurt, overwhelmed or mad and don't want to keep talking. They are the verbal equivalent of slamming the door in someone's face. Shutdown statements are your way of ending the conversation but they leave the other person without resolution. Some examples of shutdown statements are:

- "Fine" (When it's not fine)
- "Nothing" (When something is bothering you)
- "I can't do anything right"
- "It doesn't matter" (When it does matter)
- "You're right" (When you don't believe they are right)

These are all examples of shutdown statements that will immediately kill any conversation and leave the other person feeling devalued. When you shut down a conversation without resolution and without an agreed upon time to revisit the conversation, it will be difficult to ignore the unresolved issues and continue communicating as if everything was normal. Avoid shutdown statements to keep communication going.

One or all of these five communication killers may be present in your relationship. If you're like me, I tend to rotate through these depending on the current atmosphere of our marriage and my current "pettiness" level. Take some time to evaluate your current communication patterns, discuss together and create a plan for developing stronger communication.

TAKE ACTION

Watch
5 Communication Killers
on the Relationshots *YouTube* channel

1. If on a scale of 1 to 5 in the five communication killers: minimizing, defensiveness, sarcasm, universal statement and shutdown statements *(1 being needs improvement and 5 being area of strength)*. Give some specific examples of why you gave yourself that score.

2. Ask your partner which of the five communication killers they believe you engage in the most.

3. Share how you feel when your partner engages in that communication killer and how it impacts your desire to communicate.

4. Identify one thing you each will do this week to eliminate the communication killer you most need to work on.

5. Come up with a way to express to each other when you feel the other person is exhibiting their communication killer to increase recognition and hold each other accountable. You may call out the killer by name (e.g. "that's a shutdown statement") or have some other light-hearted code word you both agree on (turtle, unicorn, waterfall, etc.) that can be said when a communication killer shows up.

CHAPTER 16
IS YOUR BAGGAGE IMPACTING YOUR RELATIONSHIP?

In Chapter 1 you discovered that one of the three keys to a successful relationship is what I call personal responsibility. This simply means we all have a personal responsibility to address any personal issues that are negatively impacting our relationship. That may be past relationship wounds, unhealthy personal habits or mental health struggles. It should not be your partner's responsibility to point out or hold you accountable to personal growth and healing.

Over the past decade of working with couples, I've noticed that many couples who give up on their marriages do so not because they couldn't figure out the relational aspect of the marriage but because one or both of the spouses chose not to deal with and heal baggage they brought into the relationship. We all have baggage from our family of origin and from past relationships that will require healing and the elimination of false beliefs about ourselves and others. No one is exempt from this. It is easy to underestimate how past wounds can impact our present relationships so let me give you three truths about wounds in hopes you will fully understand the power of their impact.

1. WOUNDS WILL OVERPOWER YOUR PRIORITIES

Are you familiar with the term "retail therapy?" You may have a priority to budget and manage your money until your feelings of failure or loneliness become great enough and then next thing you know you're off to the mall or opening the front door to pick up another Amazon package. Holding down a steady job may be a priority but you just quit your third job in two years because they people there didn't "respect you" or "value you" the way you think they should.

Connecting with your partner is probably a priority for you or you wouldn't be in a relationship but I'm guessing there are some emotional triggers for you that quickly cause you to exhibit behaviors that cause disconnection or just pull away altogether. Unmanaged, these wounds will continue to prevent you from prioritizing the things that are important for the relationship.

2. WOUNDS WILL OVERPOWER YOUR BELIEFS

Have you ever professed a belief about something and then acted in a way that contradicts that belief? It could be that you just flat out lied and you don't actually believe that thing or it's probably more likely that you do believe it generally but when an area of woundedness comes into play the belief goes out the window. You might believe that physical violence is unacceptable in a relationship but then your emotions get out of hand, you aren't able to control the situation with your words or influence, that childhood wound of feeling like you never have a voice gets triggered and you decide to make sure you're heard with your hands.

Most people I know that have an affair believe that doing so is unacceptable. If they believe infidelity is wrong then why do they do it? Usually it's an unhealed wound. They may not feel good about themselves and need outside affirmation or acceptance to feel better and next thing you know, that desire for attention leads them down a road they never intended to travel. Unhealed wounds will cause us to do things contrary to what we believe.

3. WOUNDS WILL OVERPOWER YOUR THEOLOGY

For those of you who practice faith and have developed a worldview based on biblical values, you beliefs and behaviors are usually driven by your theological perspective on life and relationships. There are other times when it seems your behavior goes directly against the theology you profess. You've likely heard a story about some spiritual leader who has been embezzling money or having an affair with the secretary. How did they get there? Usually it's some area of their personal life, some past pain or wound that has never been adequately dealt with. At the crossroads of decision-making they find themselves in a conflict between their theology and covering or removing their pain. Many times the pain wins the argument and they act contrary to their theological perspective.

In working with couples I have found that "good theology" often takes a back seat to unhealed wounds. Your faith guides your values, decisions and relationships ninety percent of the time but if there are areas of unhealed woundedness you may act "out of character" in an attempt to protect your areas of shame and pain. We often don't recognize our wounds and fail to see how they are operating in our relationships so let me give you three indicators that past pain may be in the driver's seat in your relationship.

1. **Exaggerated Responses** – If your response to a statement, hurt or offense is greater than what is normal for others, a wound may be driving it.
2. **Posture of Protection** – If you find yourself guarding areas of your life and not exhibiting openness and authenticity to avoid pain or disappointment, a wound may be at work.
3. **Desire for Control** – If you attempt to control the majority of the relationship, control outcomes or control your environment, it's likely this is a way of avoiding a wound being reopened or exposed.

We have a personal responsibility to address our past wounds, to grow and to heal so our relationships aren't suffering from past hurts. Sometimes this healing can be done with your partner and other times it may require outside help or counseling.

TAKE ACTION

Watch
Dealing With Baggage in a Relationship
on the Relationshots *YouTube* channel

1. Share with your partner any areas of past relational pain that you are aware impact your current relationship. Give specific examples if you can.

2. What have you done or are presently doing to work on healing this area?

3. Share with your partner any areas of the relationship you feel are impacted by their past wounds. Give specific examples if you can.

4. Do you see any of the three indicators of past pain (exaggerated responses, posture of protection or desire for control) at work in your relationship? Give examples.

5. What is one thing you can begin doing to prevent these three indicators from negatively impacting your relationship?

CHAPTER 17
THREE THINGS THAT DAMAGE TRUST IN A RELATIONSHIP

Trust is essential for a healthy relationship. You need to trust your partner in order to feel comfortable and safe opening up, being vulnerable and expressing love. A lack of trust makes relationship extremely difficult because you begin to question intentions and motives, overthink things, overreact to things and eventually struggle to believe the relationship could ever be different. Trust is tricky because it takes time and consistency to build but can be destroyed in a moment.

There are some obvious trust breakers like unfaithfulness and dishonesty but it's often the more subtle things that ultimately end up destroying trust in most relationships. Let's look at three not-so-obvious relational issues that destroy trust.

1. CONTROL

Control in a relationship can be either overt or subtle. Overt control attempts are pretty easy to recognize and address. One person tries to prevent the other from going places or doing certain activities. Someone tries to make the other feel guilty for wanting to do things without them. Controlling behaviors such as not respecting boundaries, constant checking in, monitoring spending or reward and punishment based on performance will quickly erode trust.

One of the subtle ways individuals attempt to control their partners is through the use of questions. They can always play their real motive off as something more innocent than it really is through questions which makes it hard to address. They may say, "Do you want me to come to the store with you?" This seems like an innocent and kind question but they aren't interested in being helpful, they just don't really trust the other person and want go along to keep an eye on them. Someone might ask, "What's your new motivation to go to the gym?" when they are really just jealous and concerned their partner has someone specific at the gym they are going to see. Questions can often have the appearance of innocence but actually be a subtle way to control.

2. CRITICISM

Criticism becomes a trust killer because it puts a person in the position of second-guessing their thoughts and actions for fear of being criticized. It is impossible to relax and be yourself when you fear judgment from your partner on a regular basis and it's hard to trust someone when you question whether they have your best interest in mind. Criticism can sometimes be accidental, especially for those who ask lots of questions to gather information. Their partner may feel like the questions are a form of criticism when that isn't the intent.

For others criticism is intentional and has become the tool they use as a way to force the other person to change. They believe the other person will make adjustments to their behaviors, looks, weight, values or beliefs if they can criticize them enough. The criticisms become a form of self-protection where they attack the other person rather than being vulnerable and sharing what they really desire from them.

3. CHARACTER ISSUES

Unaddressed character issues often seem small or insignificant but over time will damage trust just like secrets and deception can. An unwillingness to communicate regularly will open the door to doubts about transparency. Procrastination can cause a person to believe their partner doesn't care about how their behavior impacts the relationship. A lack of follow through on tasks will make their significant other wonder if they can count on them to get things done. Not keeping your word can create serious trust issues around commitment to the relationship. Impulsive spending decisions can break trust around fiscal responsibility and decision-making.

As we discussed in Chapter 1, we have a personal responsibility to our partner to address our character issues that may be damaging trust in the relationship. Procrastination, lack of communication and issues with following through may not seem like obvious trust breakers but they will chip away at a person's ability to count on their partner when it matters most. It's not always the big, catastrophic events like infidelity or financial deceit but the little moments day in and day out in the relationship that slowly erodes trust.

TAKE ACTION

Watch
Enemies of Trust in a Relationship
on the Relationshots *YouTube* channel

1. Rate yourself on a scale of 1 to 5 in the three areas of control, criticism and character *(1 being needs improvement and 5 being area of strength)*.

2. Ask your partner to evaluate you in the three areas of control, criticism and character. Get some specific examples of why they gave you the rating they did.

3. Ask for some ways that your partner feels criticized by you in the relationship. You may be unaware of things you do that feel critical to them, especially when there is an absence of appreciation in the relationship. For more on that see Chapter 42.

4. Ask your partner if you have any character issues that make it difficult for them to trust you at times.

5. What is one thing you will work on this week to strengthen trust in the relationship?

CHAPTER 18

EIGHT REMINDERS OF WHAT MARRIAGE REALLY IS

There's an old saying that, "You usually see what you're looking for." Said another way, "Your perspective about your experience is more important than your experience." If you and I were to sit down and have a dialogue about the reasons you got married, we would essentially create a short or long list of what you expected and are looking for in the relationship. Ultimately, this list is what you will use to evaluate your relationship. If you happen to have a wrong view of marriage this will logically impact the way you see, experience and evaluate your relationship.

When it comes to marriage it's vitally important that we have a healthy and realistic perspective of what marriage is and is not supposed to be. If we don't, we are likely to develop resentment towards our partner for not meeting our expectations. Unfortunately, we have been given so much false information about romance and marriage that many people enter into their marriages with unhealthy and unrealistic ideas of what it should look like. Let's look at eight truths about marriage in hopes that our discussion might correct or realign any expectations that have become skewed.

1. MARRIAGE IS A GIFT

Gratitude is key to any relationship, so the moment you think the person you commit your life to now "owes you" something you will no longer see the relationship as a gift. Someone else is committing the rest of their life to you. That's a gift. None of us is so great that we deserve that level of trust. Remember marriage is a gift. Not a right. Not a burden. It's a gift!

2. MARRIAGE IS AN OPPORTUNITY TO LEARN LOVE

Despite what you may think, nobody steps into marriage fully knowledgeable and equipped to perfectly love their spouse. It's a learning process. We must teach each other how we desire to be loved and learn how our spouse receives love. Love isn't some mysterious chemical connection or feeling that overtakes us. Love is built and that takes time.

3. MARRIAGE IS AS MUCH INTERNAL AS IT IS EXTERNAL

Our inner communication with ourselves about our spouse and our marriage will affect our marriage more than our outer communication. We need to be careful and wise concerning our inner communication about our spouse and marriage. Our tendency to either believe the best or the worst about our spouse will impact how we interact with them

4. MARRIAGE IS INFLUENCED BY OUR PAST

Unresolved issues from our past have more impact on our marriage than we can accurately assess.(For more on that check out Chapter 16) The unintentional way many people date today causes them to ignore or overlook past relational wounds and instead look to the excitement of a new relationship as a way of forgetting about the last one. Personal healing and health may be one of the most important aspects of a healthy marriage.

5. MARRIAGE IS A CALL TO SERVANTHOOD

If you're not okay with serving others, marriage is definitely not for you. One of our primary goals in marriage is to look out for the best interests of our spouse. That means we desire for their life to be better before we are concerned with ourselves. We should show up on our wedding day and every day after more focused on what we can give than on what we can get.

6. MARRIAGE IS ABOUT FRIENDSHIP

Hollywood movies and romance novels celebrate and highlight sex, romance and infatuation in our romantic relationships but the strength of a marriage is not found in chemistry, romance and sex but in the strength of the friendship. When asked what the determining factor in their satisfaction with the sex, romance and passion in the marriage was, 70% of both men and women answered it was the quality of their friendship!

7. MARRIAGE REQUIRES SUFFERING

I think it's safe to say that today's couples lack the relational pain tolerance that the previous generation had, to which many of you would say, "I'm not just going to stay together and be miserable like my parents did." I'm not saying you need to stay miserable. Work on your relationship and make it better. I am saying that a life-long relationship is going to require some suffering. You will have moments of loss, moments of grieving and moments of pain. We shouldn't be surprised by this in marriage.

8. MARRIAGE IS A REFINING PROCESS

Marriage not only gives you a front row seat to your spouse's refining process but it also requires some refining in your life. That's the nature of marriage. No other relationship in your life will have the ability to mold, challenge and refine you like marriage. I thought I was selfless until I got married. I thought I was patient until I got married. I thought I was generous and loving until I got married. I thought I was laid back and easy going until I got married. The proximity and expectations a marriage relationship will place on you will expose every crack in your character and every selfish bone in your body. The refining process will burn off, chip off and sand off so many areas of your life in a way that no other relationship can.

I don't know if that list was encouraging or discouraging compared to your current expectations about marriage but I do know that these things are all true of marriage. We've been sold an unrealistic and unhealthy perspective on relationships that is hurting couples and destroying marriages. A proper perspective on marriage will allow us to step into the realities of relationship and build strong, thriving marriages.

TAKE ACTION

Watch
8 Things Nobody Told You About Marriage
on the Relationshots *YouTube* channel

1. Go through each of the eight truths with your partner and discuss how you feel about that principle.

2. Which of the eight truths makes marriage most difficult for you?

3. Which of the eight truths have you experienced to be true in your relationship?

4. Which of the eight truths do you need to grow in most?

5. What is one thing you will commit to do this week based on these truths?

CHAPTER 19
MANAGING DIFFERENCES

One of the keys to a successful relationship is a couple's ability to manage their differences. Our differences are what makes each relationship unique and our differences are what often frustrate us and cause us pain. When you commit to marriage you are signing up for a specific set of unresolvable issues. While some issues in relationship are resolvable, many of our relational struggles are what experts refer to as "perpetual problems." These differences could be around our basic needs, punctuality, organization, amount of time spent together or alone, how you relate to family, personality and preferred lifestyle to name a few. We won't fundamentally change in many of these areas, so couples must learn to manage the differences.

As you approach your differences I would encourage you to take one of two approaches. When possible, celebrate your differences. You do this by choosing to value your partner in the areas they are different from you. You appreciate those differences. You validate those differences. You focus on the moments and situations where their differences add perspective and improve things. You avoid the temptation to only highlight the ways in which their differences frustrate you.

When it becomes difficult to celebrate your differences because the level of conflict and pain associated with these differences becomes too frequent, you shift your approach from celebration to closing the gap. Closing the gap is simply making movement towards your partner in a specific area of difference to show you value them and their perspective. Let's take finances as an example. One of you is a saver and the other a spender. This gap may never fully close but you can each take one step towards the other person. The spender agrees to cut out one trip to Starbucks each week in honor of their partner and the saver agrees to eat out one time per month because that dinner together is important to their partner. Two people each take one step towards the other and close the gap of difference. The smaller the gap the less conflict that will occur. Continue closing the gap over time and a couple can minimize or even eliminate conflict in this area.

Closing the gap will require you each to both accommodate and accept one another. Accommodation is taking the steps, just mentioned, between saver and spender. Accepting is realizing that the saver will never become a spender and the spender will never fully move to the side of the saver but both can accept the other and seek to understand why they are the way they are. Accepting is a commitment to stop trying to change the person through criticism, complaint or attack. You can address specific issues that your differences cause in the relationship and seek to accommodate each other but give up the pursuit of changing the other person. It isn't going to happen and will simply increase conflict.

As you think about trying to manage your differences, here are a few common differences taken from the book *"Eight Dates"* by John and Julie Gottman, that cause conflict for couples and require a commitment to closing the gap.

1. Differences in punctuality: One person is always on time or early and the other is more casual about time and often late.

2. Differences in neatness and organization: One person may be neat and organized, while the other is more disorganized and doesn't mind a bit of mess.

3. Differences in doing tasks and getting things done: One person may be a multitasker, doing lots of things at the same time and the other likes to focus on one thing at a time.

4. Differences in emotionality: One person is very emotionally expressive and the other is not so expressive. One person might value exploring one's emotions more than the other, who believes more in action than introspection about feelings.

5. Differences in wanting time together versus time apart and alone: One person wants more time alone than the other, who wants more time together. These reflect basic differences in wanting autonomy versus interdependence.

6. Differences in sleep routine: One person stays up late while the other prefers to go to bed early and rise early. One person enjoys falling asleep with the TV on, while the other person needs quiet and dark to fall asleep.

7. Differences in optimal sexual frequency: One person wants sex more often than the other.

8. Differences in independence: One person feels a greater need to be independent versus interconnected than the other.

9. Differences in finances: One person is much more financially conservative, a worrier and a planner, while the other wants to spend a lot more than the other and has a philosophy of living for the moment.

10. Differences in how to discuss disagreements: One person wants to be able to fight openly and be as emotionally expressive as possible, while the other may require a more logical, calm, and rational approach to conflict, without much emotionality.

There are as many differences in couples as there are individuals in relationship. The quality of your connection in marriage will be tied to your ability to manage your differences in a healthy and respectful way. Celebrate these differences whenever possible and seek to close the gap when celebration becomes difficult. Accommodate and accept one another.

TAKE ACTION

Watch
Managing Differences
on the Relationshots *YouTube* channel

1. Identify three of the areas of greatest difference in your relationship.
2. What are some ways you can celebrate your differences in the relationship?
3. Which areas do you need to improve at "closing the gap" in your relationship?
4. What are some practical ways to close the gap in these areas?
5. What is one thing you will commit to do this week that can help close the gap in an area of your relationship that has caused frustration or conflict recently?

CHAPTER 20
THREE LEVELS OF BOUNDARIES

Boundaries in relationships are a necessary component for healthy interaction and an ongoing discussion we should be having in all our relationships. In Chapter 6, we defined boundaries, evaluated our boundaries and gave some practical steps in setting boundaries with others. Our boundaries determine what we are responsible for and what the other person is responsible for in a relationship. In building a healthy marriage, you will need boundaries inside your relationship and boundaries outside of the relationship. You will set and maintain boundaries with each other for the good of your relationship. You will also need to set boundaries with friends and family to guard and protect your relationship.

Many people struggle to set boundaries because they fear conflict or have experienced relationships with others who continually violate and cross boundaries. If you have relationships with others who have not had boundaries set for them in life, you can count on the fact they will fight against and push past your boundaries because they aren't used to them. You simply need to stay consistent in communicating and enforcing your boundaries. They will eventually either have to respect those boundaries or risk losing access to you.

If you struggle to set boundaries or have relationships with others who tend to fight against your boundaries, you can start a little bit subtly and build from there as you gain confidence. Here are three levels of boundaries that you can use with outside relationships.

LEVEL 1: UNSPOKEN

One of the reasons people don't set boundaries is because they fear the other person's reaction or worry that it might lead to conflict. If you struggle in this way you may want to start with an unspoken boundary. You can begin setting a boundary without the other person even knowing you are setting a boundary for them.

Let's say you have a mother who wants to call and talk to you multiple times a day or week and when she calls often says things to you or about your spouse that you don't appreciate. It may feel daunting to tell her to stop calling or to confront her by sharing how you will end the conversation and hang up if she continues to be critical. Just start with an unspoken boundary. You simply choose not to pick up the phone or answer the text right away when she reaches out. When you have some time later and feel like talking you can go ahead and call back or respond to the text. You haven't confronted her behavior with a boundary but have simply set one by choosing not to respond every time she reaches out.

LEVEL 2: SELF-FOCUSED

With a self-focused boundary you are now communicating the boundary to the other person but you have set the focus of the boundary on you rather than on them. Directing a boundary at the other person can feel confrontational or accusatory so the self-focused boundary will be more readily received by the other person.

Staying with the same scenario of the intrusive mother, the self-focused boundary would look like this. "In order to prioritize and strengthen my marriage, Kim and I have decided that between 7-10pm we are putting our phones down and focusing on our relationship. If I don't respond to a text or answer the phone during this time it is because we are guarding this time together." Now the reality is this boundary is largely to eliminate the need to answer phone calls or texts from mom but you are not telling her directly that you are avoiding her and setting this boundary for her. The focus of this boundary is you and you are setting it for the good of yourself and your relationship.

LEVEL 3: OTHER-FOCUSED

Other-focused boundaries are what we usually think of that require us to tell a person we are setting a specific boundary for them. This can feel confrontational and often causes conflict when the other person isn't used to anyone setting boundaries for them. As mentioned earlier, expect pushback when boundaries are not common for them.

Back to our mom scenario again. An other-focused boundary might sound like this. "Mom, I do not have the time or desire to talk to you three times a day so when I don't feel like talking or don't have the time, I won't be answering my phone." Another boundary might apply to the types of conversations you don't want to have. "Mom, if you are going to be critical of me or say mean things about my spouse, I will politely end the conversation and hang up." You are now specifically addressing the behavior you don't like and letting the person know what boundary you are setting when that behavior occurs.

Boundaries are healthy for you and for those you are in relationship with but since you may struggle with conflict or confrontation, you can start with level one boundaries and move your way towards level three when needed. These three levels of boundaries are useful both in your marriage and with others outside of your marriage as you seek to build strong, healthy connections with others.

TAKE ACTION

Watch
3 Levels of Boundaries
on the Relationshots *YouTube* channel

1. Discuss any relationships with family or friends where you believe healthy boundaries could guard and protect your marriage in a greater way. Name the individuals.

2. Come up with some Level 1 boundaries that would be helpful in these relationships.

3. Come up with some Level 2 boundaries that would be helpful in these relationships.

4. Come up with some Level 3 boundaries that would be helpful in these relationships.

5. Identify 1-2 specific boundaries that you are going to implement this week for the benefit of your relationship.

CHAPTER 21
FIVE THINGS EVERY MARRIAGE NEEDS

Many of the conflicts and arguments couples have in marriage are centered around their felt needs. One person believes that a specific desire or need is important for their satisfaction and enjoyment in the relationship, so they are willing to fight for it. If I were to ask you what you need in your marriage, some of you would give me a real brief list and others would have a lengthy list of desires. A significant number of these needs would be unique to you and unique to your marriage because of how you are wired and how you express and receive love.

While there are hundreds of unique desires you may be able to identify as needs for your marriage, I believe there are five things every marriage needs to be healthy and thrive. The absence of any of these five things will either cause damage to the relationship or will prevent the type of connection and intimacy necessary for a successful marriage. I encourage you to use this list as a foundation for evaluating the health of your relationship.

1. SECURITY

We all need to know that our partner's love is not going anywhere. That's one of the reasons that marriage is supposed to be a life-long covenant, so neither person has to worry about whether their spouse will stay around or not. For love to grow in a marriage, we need to know that our spouse's love for us is secure, unconditional and forever.

Security is knowing that our spouse is there for us in seasons where we're not at our best, in seasons where we fall short and in times where we are growing, developing and changing.

When couples threaten divorce or abandon each other emotionally or physically, they undermine the security in the relationship and prevent the relationship from growing.

2. ACCEPTANCE

Every one of us desperately desires to be accepted. We want to be accepted for who we are, not just what we can do or provide. Being accepted for what we do or provide will create a performance-based marriage. This is where we are always trying to measure our worthiness based on what we do and how our spouse evaluates those actions. The problem with that approach is that we all fall short at times, mess up and don't measure up to our full potential. This can lead to us hiding who really are. If we want true intimacy and love in our marriages, we need to be able to reveal our true, naked self and that will only occur if we feel accepted.

3. EMOTIONAL CONNECTION

Healthy marriages require an emotional connection. Empathy, support, care, listening, understanding and trust all create an emotional connection. We need to be able to hear and understand each other to connect emotionally. When we are present with each other emotionally it removes feelings of isolation and aloneness. This generally comes easier for women than men but we can all increase emotional connection just by being intentional.

4. MUTUAL RESPECT

Romantic love is based on equality and mutual respect. If one person dominates the relationship and the other is overly submissive and not respected, the marriage isn't going to thrive. Equality in a marriage allows each person to value the contributions, gifts, perspectives and uniqueness of the other person. You can't value your own uniqueness while criticizing your spouse's and expect a great relationship.

Mutual respect means both partners validate and respect one another both in private and public while avoiding criticisms and put-downs. When this occurs, a marriage will thrive. You can't validate and appreciate your spouse if you don't see them as an equal and worthy of the respect you desire.

5. PHYSICAL TOUCH

Whether you are a naturally affectionate person or not, human beings need to be touched. People need to be nurtured physically. The things we've already mentioned; equality, security, and acceptance are all expressed through physical touch. Holding hands, an embrace or cuddling on the couch can all communicate acceptance and security in the relationship. Non-sexual touch is essential to staying connected in marriage.

Marriages also need a fulfilling sexual relationship. Part of God's design for a couple "becoming one" is the sexual relationship. The sexual intimacy in marriage is often a reflection of the other aspects of the relationship and, like the other aspects of touch, the sexual relationship should be respectful, mutual, accepting, and secure.

You and your spouse will have a variety of desires and needs in the relationship driven by how you each give and receive love but these five needs should be a foundational focus when evaluating the quality and health of your marriage. Take some time and evaluate how you are currently doing in the areas of security, acceptance, emotional connection, mutual respect and physical touch.

TAKE ACTION

Watch
5 Things Every Marriage Needs
on the Relationshots *YouTube* channel

1. Evaluate your marriage on a scale of 1 to 5 in the areas of security, acceptance, emotional connection, mutual respect and physical touch *(1 being needs improvement and 5 being area of strength)*.

2. Give each other a couple of examples of what things make you feel more secure and less secure in the relationship.

3. Give each other a couple of examples of what things make you feel accepted and what things make you feel rejected.

4. Give each other a couple of examples of what makes you feel emotionally connected.

5. Give each other a couple of examples of what makes you feel respected and disrespected.

6. Give each other a couple of examples of what types of physical touch you desire.

7. Share with your spouse in which of the five areas you would like to see more intentional effort. Give some specific examples of what that would look like for you.

8. What is one thing you will commit to do this week to strengthen one of these five areas?

CHAPTER 22

THREE QUESTIONS TO EMOTIONALLY CONNECT WITH YOUR SPOUSE

Disconnection is something that will just naturally show up in your relationship. You don't have to work at it, plan for it or schedule it. It is the guaranteed result of not taking the time to intentionally connect with each other. Some couples simply don't make the effort to connect and other couples want to connect but just don't know how to do it. I believe that staying connected doesn't have to be mysterious and doesn't even require much time or effort. Connection is about communication. If you ask each other the following three questions on a regular basis, I can promise you will stay connected in your relationship.

1. THE EMPATHY QUESTION: WHAT ARE YOUR GREATEST STRESSORS RIGHT NOW?

Ask your spouse this question and then listen. That's it. Allow them to share with you the things at home, the people at work, the expectations their family puts on them and the expectation of perfectionism they place on themselves. Husbands, if your wife has been telling you that you don't hear, understand her or care about her, this one question will single-handedly solve that riddle for you. Wives, your husbands need this type of support as well. They may not readily share with you all the things that are causing them stress in life but they are there and I can almost guarantee they don't have any male friends checking in on their emotional well-being.

The goal of this question is emotional connection and empathy. You are not seeking to solve all the issues they share. Offering intellectual solutions to their problems will probably not feel like emotionally connection to them. You are seeking to hear and understand the things that are causing them stress.

2. THE SUPPORT QUESTION: WHAT IS ONE THING I CAN DO TO TAKE SOME WEIGHT OFF YOUR SHOULDERS?

If I had to pick only one question to ask your spouse on a regular basis, this would be it. One of the most frustrating things to occur in a relationship is when you feel like you are making efforts and trying hard to help the other person out only to be told, "You never do anything to help me." It's easy to want to give up trying at all when you get that kind of response, especially when you have genuinely been putting in effort.

The support question is key because it ensures that the "something" you are doing is the "right thing" in your spouse's mind. For example, I could spend three hours cleaning the house but probably won't get any recognition for my efforts if my wife really needs me to help the kids finish their homework. Don't assume you know what would be most helpful when you can ask your spouse what task or activity would be most important to them at this time. Different seasons of marriage will call for different types of support so this question will need to be asked often as the answer will change.

3. THE PRIORITY QUESTION: WHAT CAN I DO THAT MAKES YOU FEEL I CARE?

We all want to feel like we are a priority to our spouse. Work, parenting, hobbies and extended family can become so time consuming that connecting with your spouse becomes an afterthought. Much like the support question, you may think you are loving and caring for your spouse but if it's not the primary way in which they want to be cared for, it may be wasted effort. You are probably not wired like your spouse so don't assume what you need most is what they desire. Ask this question to get some specific things you can be doing to make them feel like they are a priority. A second part to the priority question could be to also ask, "What do I do that makes you feel like you are not a priority?" You may be unaware of some of the behaviors that make your spouse feel like they only get whatever you have left over after focusing on your primary priorities.

If your connection has been suffering due to busyness of schedule or a lack of understanding of what creates the most connection, implement these three questions with each other on a weekly basis. If you find that three questions gives you more to focus on than you have hours in the day, pick one question each that you would like your spouse to check in with on a weekly basis.

TAKE ACTION

Watch
How to Emotionally Connect With Your Spouse
on the Relationshots *YouTube* channel

1. Ask each other The Empathy Question and simply listen to the answer. Avoid trying to solve the stressors but ask clarifying questions if you need additional information to fully understand.

2. Ask each other The Support Question.

3. Ask each other The Priority Question.

4. Which question would be most important to you and why?

5. What is one thing you will commit to doing this week based on your spouse's answer to one of the three questions?

6. Decide on a day and time each week when you will take a few minutes to ask these questions. Be intentional and make it a habit.

CHAPTER 23
MANAGING THE MOMENT

I'm guessing you have had a conflict in your relationship at some point that started off with one of you mentioning a fairly simple issue but somehow it quickly escalated and turned into a way bigger issue than either of you could have imagined. It may have even reached the point where so many other issues were brought into the conversation that you weren't exactly sure what the original issue was. Don't feel bad; we've all been there. It only takes one word, one accusation or one trigger to quickly blow up a simple conversation. The good news is, this is a very simple fix. I know you may be rolling your eyes at my assertion that your cycles of conflict and blowups can be resolved in a simple way but stay with me for a couple of minutes.

When I lead marriage classes, we always spend a little time talking about a concept I call "Managing the Moment." I believe that couples who learn to manage key moments in their relationships can greatly minimize and even eliminate many of the arguments that plague them. Let me give you a truth to memorize and then I'll break down what this looks like in your relationship: **At the moment an issue is raised in your relationship, validation is more important than truth.**

Here's what happens when we don't follow this principle. Your spouse comes to you and expresses a frustration with you leaving your dishes in the sink rather than putting them in the dishwasher. At that very moment your only goal should be to validate their concern but what normally happens is you respond with your "truth" about what has been presented. You may respond with, "You leave your dishes in the sink too." You may say, "I almost always put them in the dishwasher but the dishwasher was clean and I was in a rush this morning." You might even bring another issue into the conversation by replying, "You leave your clothes on the floor in the bathroom and I pick them up without saying anything to you." All of these statements may be true but none is important in that moment. Remember, validation is more important than truth in the moment.

Validating your spouse means you respond by acknowledging their concern and showing that you care about what has been presented to you. Your response should be something like, "I'm sorry, I'll work on that." You aren't replying with your perspective or truth about what has been presented to you but are simply validating their concern. This is very simple and anyone can do it. The fear in your head right now is probably telling you that if you validate their concern and don't also respond with the truth, your spouse will not recognize how they do the same thing. Instead, they will continue to hold you accountable for things for which they won't also receive accountability. Don't worry, I didn't say the truth isn't important at all. I said the truth isn't important "in that moment."

Going back to the dishes in the sink scenario for a moment. If it is true that your spouse leaves their dishes in the sink often and you put them in the dishwasher without saying anything, being confronted about leaving your dishes in the sink can be frustrating. I believe you can and should say something about this, just not at the moment they bring the issue to you. Maybe later that night, the next day or at an upcoming weekly staff meeting if you have one, you can bring up your truth. (See Chapter 38 for more on staff meetings) You could say something like, "Yesterday you mentioned the issue of me leaving my dishes in the sink. I hear you and will definitely work on that but it was also frustrating for you to get onto me about that because I feel like you often leave your dishes in the sink as well." Your truth will always be better received when you bring it up at a different moment. When you have already validated your spouse around their concern, they will be way more likely to want to hear what you have to say as well.

I believe conflicts succeed or fail based on how we manage the very moment the issue is raised. Validation first, truth second. Focus on validating your spouse's concerns and they will be more receptive to your truth when brought up at a later time. **At the moment an issue is raised in your relationship, validation is more important than truth.**

TAKE ACTION

Watch
Eliminate Arguments Today by "Managing the Moment"
on the Relationshots *YouTube* channel

1. Ask your spouse what types of responses would feel like validation to them so you are clear on how to express validation and understanding when they engage with you. *(For example: when I share about a concern I have in the relationship I would like you to respond with "I hear you. I'll work on that.")*

2. Ask your spouse what types of responses feel invalidating or dismissive to them.

3. Think through a recent argument that escalated and replay it with your spouse but this time respond by validating the concern rather than getting defensive or offering a counter point.

4. Commit this week to validation first in every moment where an issue is brought to you. If you don't know how or when to bring it up again and share your truth, consider implementing a weekly staff meeting. *(More on that in Chapter 38)*

CHAPTER 24
HOW TO COMPROMISE

Every relationship requires moments of compromise. In fact, I would say you can't have a healthy relationship without both partners being willing to compromise at times. You and your spouse are not identical images of each other so you will have different ideas, opinions and perspectives on many things throughout the course of your marriage. People often throw out the phrase, "A happy marriage is a union of two good forgivers." I would say a successful marriage is the union of two great compromisers. If you always want things your way, marriage is going to be a tough relationship to manage. While compromise is key to relationship, I notice a lot of couples struggling to compromise because they believe the only type of compromise is the fifty-fifty, meet-in-the-middle compromise and many times this isn't possible.

Compromise can take many forms; I'd like to present five types of compromise that may be useful to you when trying to manage your different desires in the relationship.

1. SPLIT THE DIFFERENCE

This is the 50/50, meet-in-the-middle compromise we most often associate with the word compromise. This approach says, "I'll take one step towards you if you take one step towards me." You like the thermostat set at 74 degrees and your spouse likes it at 70 degrees. You agree to set the thermostat at 72 degrees so you both feel like you've given equally.

This approach can help manage differences in spending, extroversion and introversion, how long you stay at the in-laws and eating out but may not work in all situations. In fact, whole books have been written on the subject of "never splitting the differences" in business negotiations; people have strong opinions on this approach. It can be helpful in certain situations.

2. IF YOU DO THIS FOR ME, I'LL DO THAT FOR YOU

Let me give you a quick disclaimer before I describe this one. The motivation on this compromise is to add value to or help your spouse, not for you to get your way. If your motivation is selfish, you will become resentful if you feel like the reciprocation didn't measure up to your contribution. "If you can grab my dry cleaning on your way home, I'll grab dinner tonight." The goal is for you both to accomplish some things that need to be done and taking something off your spouse's to-do list allowed them to grab dinner for the family. It can also be used as a way to support each other's desires when their wants aren't on the top of your list. "If you come to the basketball game with me, I'll watch the Hallmark movie with you when we get home." The goal is time together and the compromise is to each step into the other's world to connect.

3. MY WAY THIS TIME, NEXT TIME YOU CHOOSE

When you both can't have what you desire in the same decision, this compromise can be useful. This approach could help solve the "where to eat dinner" dilemma. You want Mexican food and your spouse wants a good steak. "Let's go grab a steak tonight and then next time we'll have Mexican food." You can use this compromise to resolve differences in where to vacation, go out to eat, spend discretionary income or whose family you spend the holidays with.

4. PART OF WHAT I WANT AND PART OF WHAT YOU WANT

This compromise can be a really effective approach when you are willing to communicate and understand why your spouse desires the things they do. Most couples use this approach when purchasing a house or car. You want a large kitchen to cook and entertain and your spouse wants a big backyard for the kids, so you look for a house that has both. There may be other things about the house that wouldn't necessarily be your priority but if you are able to get the things most important to you, compromising in other areas isn't a big deal. You might also use this approach in purchasing a car. You want heated seats and your spouse wants a specific color. It might not be the color you would choose but you're willing to compromise there as long as it has heated seats for the winter.

5. THE TEMPORARY TRY

When it's not possible to each give a little or for both of you to get some of what you each want, the temporary try can be your friend. The temporary try says, "Try it my way for two weeks and if you don't like it, then we can try it your way." One of you may want to do something new and the other thinks the current approach is fine. You agree to try it for a couple of weeks and if things haven't improved you go back to the old way. Changes don't have to be forever. You can try something new for a while and then adjust if it isn't producing the results you both desired.

As you can see, a meet-in-the-middle compromise isn't always practical or possible so consider other approaches to managing your different desires in the relationship. As you seek compromise let me give you three tips to help you succeed in this vital aspect of your marriage.

1. Keep a long-term perspective: A focus on the big picture for your relationship will keep you from getting caught up in feeling like you're "losing" in the moment when you may be making a compromise.

2. Put yourself in the other person's shoes: Learning to be empathetic is key to compromise. You must have a desire to understand why your spouse's perspective is important to them.

3. Consider the third option: We can get stuck in conflict when we believe the only two outcomes are my way or your way. Compromise isn't always "yours" or "mine." As you have seen with the five types of compromise, there is often a third option.

TAKE ACTION

Watch
How to Compromise in Relationships
on the Relationshots *YouTube* channel

1. Which of the five types of compromise was a new approach for you? How do you feel about that approach?

2. What makes compromise difficult for you in your relationship? *(Not getting what you want, feeling controlled by your spouse, fear that compromising will become one-sided, etc.)*

3. Think about a recent conflict of interests you had in your marriage and identify which type of compromise you used. Now brainstorm another solution using one of the different approaches to compromise.

4. Discuss a compromise you have made in the relationship that you don't feel good about. *(Maybe you feel it was unfair. Maybe you don't like how the compromise has worked out even though it sounded like a good idea.)* Come up with another approach to the compromise that you can try for a while to see if you both feel good about it.

CHAPTER 25

MYTHS ABOUT MARRIAGE – PART 1

I don't know about you but over the almost three decades of my marriage there have been many moments I've said to myself, "Why didn't anybody tell me this is what marriage looked like?" There are things about marriage that we didn't know to be ready for and there are myths about marriage that romance novels and romantic movies have deceived us into believing. Having unrealistic expectations about marriage will only set us up for failure as disappointment and hopelessness begin to set in around these unmet expectations. In this chapter and the next, I want to give you thirteen myths about marriage that may be giving you unrealistic expectations and causing you to experience unnecessary resentment. Let's adjust our mindset by busting these unhelpful myths.

MYTH #1: I CAN CHANGE THE PERSON AFTER WE MARRY

Most of us don't believe we can fundamentally change who our spouse is but if we're honest, a lot of us think we can influence some aspects of their character, habits or preferences once we are married and together day and night. If we just apply enough pressure, criticism or punishment then surely, they'll adapt to please us, right? Wrong. In a healthy marriage we do influence one another but the one thing you'll never be in control of in your relationship is your spouse.

MYTH #2: MARRIAGE WILL FIX SOME OF OUR ISSUES

In the dating process it's easy to look ahead to marriage and believe that the marriage commitment and daily proximity will fix some of the frustrations and issues you are dealing with because you are not yet "one." It's possible that marriage might help resolve some of your issues but I can guarantee that it will also create new issues not present in dating. It's also true that many of your issues will not only continue but actually increase. When looking at the transition from dating to marriage, the truth is that the good doesn't always last and the bad often becomes worse.

MYTH #3: MARRIAGE WILL SATISFY SOME OF MY PERSONAL ISSUES

We all bring personal baggage into our marriages and it's easy to believe that marriage will help us with these issues. (See Chapter 16 for a discussion on baggage). I know people who have been unfaithful in their relationships while dating but somehow are convinced that once they're married this will no longer be a temptation or issue. I know people who have pornography or masturbation addictions that believe the sexual relationship in marriage will satisfy all their desires in this area of sexuality. I know people with spending issues that believe some accountability from their spouse will somehow resolve the root issues driving their spending. The truth is marriage tends to magnify not satisfy our personal issues.

MYTH #4: WE MARRY OUR SPOUSE NOT THEIR FAMILY

Go ahead, have a good laugh along with me. If you've been married longer than two weeks, you already know this isn't true. If you live in a Western culture, independence is a core value. Many Eastern cultures with rich family traditions would never buy into this myth because family is usually heavily involved in the mate selection process. In Western cultures the focus on love and passion has led many to believe that the goal is "me and you" against the world: "If I've got you then I don't need anybody else." The reality of marriage is your relationship will include family influence. Even if you don't spend much time around extended family, your spouse has beliefs, traditions and perspectives on relationship highly influenced by their family, so you are indeed marrying their family in many ways.

MYTH #5: THERE IS "THE ONE" YOU SHOULD MARRY

If you still believe that a happy, successful marriage is about finding your "soulmate" let me disappoint you. Soulmates aren't some biblical principle or mandate; they are mythological creatures. Seriously, the idea of finding your soulmate comes from Greek mythology. According to Greek mythology, humans were originally created with four arms, four legs and head with two faces. Zeus supposedly feared their power, so he split them into two separate parts, condemning them to spend the rest of their lives searching for their other halves. Marriage is a choice to commit yourself to another person, not the culmination of finding "the one."

Many of you feel like you've found your soulmate because this relationship feels different from any other you've had. Congratulations! I'm glad you have found the person you believe to be your soulmate. Others of you don't always feel that confident about your marriage and wonder if your soulmate is out there somewhere. They aren't. They are right in front of you. Your marriage will be as good as the intentional effort you decide to put into it.

MYTH #6: FOLLOW YOUR HEART

Our emotions aren't consistent and our feelings are fleeting. There might be no worse advice than to follow your heart. That journey will take you to places you don't belong, have you doing things you shouldn't be doing and cause you to believe things that aren't true. I'm not discounting our emotions but I am suggesting that we approach our relationships with both our head and our heart. Healthy marriages will require us to do things, at times, that we just don't want to do. Love is an action not a feeling. When your heart and head align, absolutely follow your heart. Allowing your heart to lead your decision-making on a regular basis will lead to unhealthy relationships and erratic behavior.

MYTH #7: HAPPINESS IS THE GOAL OF MARRIAGE

This myth may be the greatest reason for divorce. Since the passing of "no fault divorce" by Governor Ronald Reagan in 1969, people have been ending their marriages because they just aren't happy anymore. Citing "irreconcilable differences," couples depart an unhappy situation in search of fulfillment and happiness. If the goal of your marriage is your happiness, you will frequently want to end the relationship. The reason you marry will likely be the driver for your divorce. If you marry for happiness and fulfillment, the absence of these will cause you to evaluate the marriage as unsuccessful. If you married for financial gain and your spouse loses their job, you'll question the relationship. If you married for children and face infertility issues, you'll question the relationship. Happiness may be an outcome of a strong, healthy marriage but can't be the goal.

You may be shaking the book at this point asking where this was before you got married. I guess you should have called me then! Be encouraged, it's never too late. Replacing any of these lies you have believed to be true will actually set you free from the bondage of that myth and allow you to operate in truth. This will help you to shift unrealistic expectations and focus on the things that actually lead to a great marriage. If you've got friends who are not yet married, be a great friend. Buy them a copy of this book and make it required premarital reading.

TAKE ACTION

Watch
Marriage Myths: 13 Lies We Believe About Marriage – Part 1
on the Relationshots *YouTube* channel

1. Which of the seven myths were you guilty of believing prior to marriage?

2. Which of the seven myths do you still believe? How do you feel about it after reading this chapter?

3. Which of the seven myths have led to issues in the relationship due to unhealthy expectations? Give some specific examples of behaviors or mindsets.

4. What is one thing you will commit to doing differently this week in response to replacing the myth with truth?

CHAPTER 26

MYTHS ABOUT MARRIAGE - PART 2

If you haven't yet read Chapter 25, turn back a couple of pages and start with the first seven myths about marriage. Hopefully, those weren't too painful for you. Now, let's jump in with myths eight through thirteen.

MYTH #8: DON'T GO TO BED ANGRY

Many Christians love to support this myth with scripture. Ephesians 4:26-27 says, "In your anger do not sin: do not let the sun go down while you are still angry, and do not give the devil a foothold." See, Eric, you are telling us the Bible is a myth and not to believe it. There you go jumping to extremes again. These verses present a great principle but this is not an absolute command that we can remove from all context and make it an unwavering rule. The principle is that a habit of not dealing with conflict or finding resolution but continuing to put it off, will ultimately build resentment and bitterness in the relationship.

Sometimes in your relationship, you won't be able to resolve your issues that night and staying up all night trying to do so will only cause more anger and damage. In these cases, you will need to agree upon a time in the near future to revisit the issue and then get some sleep. Nobody becomes more logical or effective the more tired they become.

MYTH #9: YOUR SPOUSE MUST BE YOUR BEST FRIEND

You may be thinking to yourself, "The further we go in these myths the more extreme this guy gets. Now, he's telling me not to be friends with my spouse." I am not proposing that friendship isn't important in marriage, I'm simply presenting that the idea your spouse has to be your best friend may not be possible for everyone. I do believe that friendship with your spouse is vital to the health of your marriage and if you're looking to grow your friendship see Chapter 8 for how to grow your friendship in marriage. For some couples, their personality differences, hobbies and lifestyle preferences may be different enough that they don't spend a lot of time together recreationally, but still maintain a healthy connection. In these cases, it may be that your spouse isn't the person you do a lot of activities with or have conversations with regularly about your most passionate hobbies. Your spouse should be one of your closest friends but may not be your best friend in this context.

MYTH #10: CHILDREN WILL MAKE THE MARRIAGE STRONGER

A lot of couples believe that a common purpose, parenting, will unite them and make them stronger. This isn't usually the case because many couples parent in drastically different ways. This means our parenting challenges will cause more division than they do unity. Children will also look for ways to play parents against each other in order to get what they want. If dad says no, they'll simply go ask mom looking for a different response. For more on this topic check out Chapter 39: Marriage Killers.

MYTH #11: HEALTHY COUPLES ALWAYS WANT TO DO STUFF TOGETHER

It's important and healthy for couples to enjoy time together, but it doesn't have to be everything. Are there some couples that genuinely love spending all their free time together? Absolutely, but that doesn't mean that every couple should feel this way. Many couples enjoy both time together and time apart and there is nothing wrong with that. This may be influenced by what they each enjoy doing and by their attachment style. (See Chapters 5, 27 and

28 for more on attachment style) The key to healthy connection is making sure that you are finding enough things to do together to build your friendship and avoid the trap of disconnection by living completely separate lives.

MYTH #12: YOU SHOULD BE ABLE TO RESOLVE ALL YOUR CONFLICTS

Relationship experts have found that the majority of issues in marriage are unresolvable. They refer to these issues as "perpetual problems." These may center around our personalities, lifestyle preferences and desires. Too many couples spend energy in conflict trying to resolve issues that are unresolvable. Marriage is about resolving the issues that can be resolved while managing the differences that can't be resolved. A belief that all issues can and must be resolved will lead to great frustration and hopelessness. For more on how to manage our unresolvable issues check out Chapter 19.

MYTH #13: YOUR SPOUSE SHOULD "COMPLETE" YOU

I shouldn't need to spend much time on this myth at this point in our conversation. Much like the elusive "soulmate" search, trying to find completion through something or someone outside of yourself is a setup for failure. We must be whole and healthy individuals before we get married. Dependence on another person to fill the areas of need in our lives will create a power dynamic where we become angry, controlling and resentful when they aren't meeting our needs in a way that satisfies us. You should be complete without your spouse and allow their presence in your life to add value and compliment you, not complete you.

Take a deep breath. You made it. Thirteen myths about marriage that the world sells and many of us have bought. Every one of these myths will lead to unhealthy, unrealistic and unmet expectations in your marriage. Replacing these myths with truth will lead to a healthy, realistic approach to your relationship. A proper perspective of marriage will allow you to accept the realities and focus on what's most important.

TAKE ACTION

Watch
13 Lies We Believe About Marriage – Part 2
on the Relationshots *YouTube* channel

1. Which of the six myths were you guilty of believing prior to marriage?

2. Which of the six myths do you still believe? How do you feel about it after reading this chapter?

3. Which of the six myths have led to issues in the relationship due to unhealthy expectations? Give some specific examples of behaviors or mindsets.

4. What is one thing you will commit to doing differently this week in response to replacing the myth with truth?

CHAPTER 27

SEVEN TRIGGERS FOR THOSE WITH AVOIDANT ATTACHMENT STYLE

If you're not yet familiar with attachment styles, check out Chapter 5 on "Understanding Your Attachment Style" to get an overview of the four styles associated with Attachment Theory. As a reminder, attachment style is simply the way a person has learned to connect in relationships, influenced by their early relationship with caregivers. If you or your spouse have identified with the avoidant attachment style, it will be important for you both to understand what can trigger this style. If not, you will likely experience the frustrating cycle where the non-avoidant spouse pushes for greater connection causing the avoidant spouse to withdraw or create space and that cycle repeats.

Those with avoidant attachment styles value independence and freedom and can often be uncomfortable depending on others or feeling like their partner is too dependent upon them. They are generally self-sufficient and don't desire as much intimacy as their spouse typically does. That means anyone with an avoidant partner can feel like the quest for connection and intimacy has become a confusing journey of two steps towards greater connection followed by one step backwards. Here are seven triggers that can cause an avoidant partner to pull away so you can recognize and avoid these hindrances to intimacy.

1. BEING CRITICIZED BY SOMEONE THEY LOVE

Because they are uncomfortable with closeness, allowing someone in emotionally is a big deal. If they allow this level of intimacy and receive constant criticism in response, they will tend to pull away again.

2. THEIR SPOUSE DEMANDING ATTENTION

The key word here is "demand." If you demand attention from an avoidant partner expect them to retreat. You can request it, appeal for it or share your desire for it but don't demand something they aren't naturally comfortable with or interested in.

3. HAVING TO DEPEND ON SOMEONE

Depending on others is difficult for an avoidant partner so being forced into a situation where they have to depend on someone will often be triggering. If they have to depend on you for something, which is likely in a marriage, avoid using this dependence as a tool to remind them or manipulate them later on down the road. If you approach them with a "you owe me because of what I did for you" posture, they'll never ask you for another thing the rest of your relationship.

4. SPOUSE WANTING TOO MUCH CLOSENESS

Remember, they value independence and enjoy space. A spouse who wants too much closeness will feel clingy and smothering, causing them to withdraw even more. It's okay to express a desire for closeness, as long as you also value and respect their need for space in the same conversation, seeking to find a solution that satisfies you both.

5. BEING JUDGED FOR BEING EMOTIONAL

Being emotional and expressing feelings is not something that comes naturally for avoidant partners. If you criticize or judge them when they do attempt to be more emotionally open or vulnerable, they will quickly shut down that part of themselves.

6. SPOUSE BECOMING TOO EMOTIONAL

You may be comfortable with lots of emotional expression and vulnerability but an avoidant spouse usually isn't. Most people feel obligated to reciprocate emotional sharing, so if you become too emotional, they may feel the pressure to match that expression and can pull back to avoid feeling overwhelmed.

7. RELATIONSHIP EXPECTATIONS CONSUMING ALL THEIR TIME

It feels like we're being redundant here but avoidants value independence and time alone. If they feel the responsibilities of the relationship are taking up too much time and preventing them from much needed alone time to decompress and refresh, they will pull away.

The goal in discussing triggers is to create language that both spouses can use to communicate about their different needs for closeness and intimacy. We often don't recognize when we're being triggered and how we might be triggering each other, hopefully these seven triggers will increase awareness when connection seems difficult.

TAKE ACTION

Watch
7 Triggers for Those With Avoidant Attachment Style
on the Relationshots *YouTube* channel

1. Share with each other which of the seven triggers you have experienced in your relationship. Give specific examples of what that looks like and how it makes you feel.

2. For the "non-avoidant": Ask your spouse how they would like for you to express a desire for more closeness.

3. For the "avoidant": Ask your spouse how you can communicate a need for space without making them feel rejection.

4. What is one thing you each can commit to doing this week to avoid these avoidant triggers?

CHAPTER 28

SEVEN TRIGGERS FOR THOSE WITH ANXIOUS ATTACHMENT STYLE

I'll just assume you've already read Chapter 5 on attachment styles and likely the previous chapter on avoidant attachment. Now, let's talk about anxious attachment and the things that trigger those with this attachment style. An anxious attachment style usually develops when there has been an inconsistent response to a child's needs, leaving them confused and stressed about whether they will be comforted or ignored when in need. This tends to "hyper-activate" their attachment system causing them to be "needy," often looking for proximity and reassurance. As adults, people with anxious attachment style tend to be clingy to their partners, have a high need for their partner's approval and constantly desire reassurance that their partner won't leave.

If this describes you or your spouse, it's important to understand what triggers someone with an anxious attachment style so you can eliminate or minimize these triggers in your relationship. Here are seven things that may trigger an anxious partner.

1. BEING INCONSISTENT

When a spouse is acting hot and cold it can trigger the anxiety because inconsistency feels unstable. If you say you'll call or do something but then don't or say you appreciate honesty but get mad when your partner tells you the truth, this can be triggering. Any behavior that creates uncertainty with someone who is already uncertain may be a trigger.

2. DISTANCE

If you've read Chapter 27 on the avoidant attachment triggers you can probably picture a setup for conflict on this one. The avoidant likes distance but distance can be triggering to an anxious spouse. For someone who desires closeness and intimacy, distance will be a trigger. Examples of distance are: not calling back, replying to texts later than usual, not checking in and being on the phone or distracted by television when you're with your spouse. Anything that threatens closeness will activate the anxiety.

3. BEING DISMISSIVE

Those with an anxious attachment style need reassurance and consistent love to feel safe. If a partner is emotionally unavailable or dismissive it will be triggering. They will begin to create narratives about why the other person isn't available or present and fear the stability of the relationship.

4. ANGER

No, I'm not saying that you can never be upset if you are in a relationship with an anxious spouse. That's not a realistic expectation. I am saying that how a person with a secure attachment and one with an anxious attachment manage anger is completely different. For someone with anxious attachment, even moderate and justified anger can trigger their stressed-out nervous system and cause them to go into fight or flight mode. They may panic, feel blamed, worry about the state of the relationship and react. Reassurance about the relationship can help minimize how anger may trigger them.

5. REJECTION

This may be the number one trigger for an anxious partner. Rejection is usually one of the reasons the person developed an anxious attachment style to begin with. If this has been a theme in their life, their nervous system will respond to even small signs of rejection even if it isn't personal.

6. HIGH EXPECTATIONS

Don't read this and conclude there can be no expectations. That would not produce a healthy relationship. Anxious partners have a high desire to please their spouse and make them happy so they aren't worried about being abandoned. If they feel like their spouse's expectations are so high that they may not be able to meet them, it can trigger their fears about the stability of the relationship. If you combine high expectations with low or absent nurturing and reassurance, expect the anxious partner to be highly triggered.

7. SPOUSE EXPRESSING INDEPENDENCE

Those with an anxious attachment style will usually want lots of time together with their spouse so when a desire for some "me time" is expressed, the anxious spouse will be triggered. They can begin to make up reasons in their head for why their partner doesn't want to be with them and will see the separate time as a threat to the relationship.

The degree of triggering that a specific event or interaction causes will depend on each person, each relationship and the current level of connection and intimacy in the relationship. It may be that some of these triggers are more significant for some than others. The key to relationship with an anxious partner is how commitment is communicated. Regular reassurance and connection will greatly decrease all of these triggers and over time help an anxious spouse move towards a more secure attachment style.

TAKE ACTION

Watch
7 Triggers for Those With Anxious Attachment Style
on the Relationshots *YouTube* channel

1. Share with each other which of the seven triggers you have experienced in your relationship. Give specific examples of what that looks like and how it makes you feel.

2. For the "non-anxious": Ask your spouse how they would like for you to express reassurance and commitment to the relationship.

3. For the "anxious": Ask your spouse how you can communicate a need for closeness without making them feel smothered.

4. What is one thing you each can commit to doing this week to avoid these anxious triggers?

CHAPTER 29
SACRIFICE IS A BAD MARRIAGE STRATEGY

Sacrificing one's own interests for the interests of someone you love is a time-honored solution to many problems in life. Many people view sacrificing for your spouse as a healthy approach to marriage and the ultimate show of care and love. The more two people give sacrificially the more ideal their marriage is, right? Maybe not. I don't think you would argue with me if I said it feels pretty good when your spouse makes a sacrifice on your behalf. Who doesn't like that? That's usually a pretty good indication they care about you and want what's best for you. I believe that a good thing can sometimes become a bad thing, so let me explain my perspective on sacrifice as a marriage strategy.

Are you familiar with the short story, *The Gift of the Magi* by O. Henry? It's a story about a poor couple that wants to give each other gifts for Christmas but don't have the money. The wife wants to give her husband a watch fob to go with his prized possession which is his watch. The husband wants to give the wife a comb for her prized possession which is her hair. The husband decides to sell his watch to get his wife a comb for her hair and she sells her hair to get him a watch fob. A beautiful story of sacrificial love with a sad and ironic ending.

Sacrifice is not always a winning strategy in marriage. Sacrifice isn't a bad thing but can have several pitfalls as a marriage strategy. Let's look at three reasons sacrifice can be a bad strategy for marriage as presented by author Dr. Willard Harley. [3]

1. SACRIFICE IS USUALLY DONE IN SECRET

As with the Gift of the Magi story, neither spouse told the other what they were doing to sacrifice. They just did it. Instead of a couple working together on a solution to a problem, sacrifice often leads to both working separately keeping their plans to themselves. Other times personal sacrifice for the sake of someone you care for means that you don't reveal your true feelings about something and instead just opt for making a sacrifice in silence. Sacrifice can prevent openness in marriage.

2. SACRIFICE DOESN'T USUALLY LEAD TO LONG-TERM SOLUTIONS

At best, sacrifice can usually only be done for a short period of time because the sacrificing spouse isn't willing to make it a habit. When one spouse's gain becomes the other spouse's voluntary loss, what was voluntary one day easily turns into an expectation that's demanded the next day. You sacrifice a few times for your spouse and because they aren't aware it's a sacrifice for you, it becomes an expectation for them.

You see this dynamic happen often in the area of sex. If on a special occasion one spouse decides to sacrifice their enjoyment and have sex the way their spouse wants to, eventually that spouse pressures them to do it again the next time, and the next time and they keep giving in. At some point the sacrificing spouse may avoid sex because it is never done in a way that is enjoyable to them. Now listen, I'm not saying we don't sacrifice for each other on occasion, I'm just explaining how it can become an expectation rather than a voluntary sacrifice.

---

[3] Willard Harley, "What is Sacrifice, and Should It Be Given In Marriage," Marriage Builders, https://www.marriagebuilders.com/what-is-sacrifice-and-should-it-be-used-in-marriage.htm.

3. SACRIFICE USUALLY EXPECTS RECIPROCATION

If I do something unpleasant so my wife can have what she wants, I'll usually be waiting for her to return the favor at some point. In fact, it can easily become a situation where the primary reason I sacrifice for my wife is only so that I can get my way in another area. If I perceive at some point that I am the only one making sacrifices, I will assume my wife doesn't care about me and will become resentful. Because sacrifice is usually done in secret my wife probably isn't even aware that I'm making the sacrifice and keeping score. This is a recipe for bitterness and resentment. It would be a very rare situation if you were able to continually sacrifice for your spouse never expecting anything in return.

If sacrifice can lead to bitterness, resentment and lopsided contributions to a marriage, is there a place for sacrifice at all? Dr. Willard Harley believes that "joint sacrifice" is preferable to "individual sacrifice" in marriage. Joint sacrifice is not done in secret but in the open with both spouse's knowing what is involved. Joint sacrifice has a defined ending and isn't expected to last indefinitely. Joint sacrifice is mutually agreed upon, requires joint effort and benefits both individuals. An example of joint sacrifice might involve both of you giving a little. If you and your spouse have different bed routines, you may each agree to follow the other person's preferred bedtime twice per week to maintain connection before bed. [4]

There may be times when individual sacrifices are made in marriage and that's okay. As a marriage strategy, however, joint sacrifice will create a happier, healthier relationship.

---

4 Willard Harley, "He Wins She Wins," (Grand Rapids, MI: Revell, 2013) 28.

TAKE ACTION

Watch
Sacrifice is a Bad Marriage Strategy
on the Relationshots *YouTube* channel

1. Discuss with your spouse some sacrifices you believe you make in secret.

2. Do you find yourself becoming resentful for sacrifices you aren't recognized for or aren't reciprocated? Give some examples.

3. What is one area of the relationship you would like to discuss how a joint sacrifice could be helpful for both of you and beneficial to the marriage?

4. What joint sacrifice will you commit to implement this week?

CHAPTER 30

SHOULD MARRIED COUPLES HAVE FRIENDS OF THE OPPOSITE SEX?

One issue that comes up over and over again in couples counseling is conflict over friendships of the opposite sex. Can married couples have friends of the opposite sex? Is it healthy to have friends of the opposite sex? Should there be rules and boundaries with friends of the opposite sex? If there is mutual trust in a marriage, does it even matter? As you can probably guess, I've got some thoughts on this subject and I believe opposite sex friendships can greatly impact a marriage.

When I talk with couples about this subject, there is a wide range of views on opposite sex friends. Here are a few of the common views I hear on this subject:

- I don't have a problem with it because if we have honest communication and trust there is nothing to worry about.
- If they've been friends long before we met, I shouldn't ask them to stop the friendship.
- As long as it isn't someone they've dated before I'm okay with it.
- As long as it isn't someone they've been sexually intimate with I'm okay with it.
- If they introduce me to the person and I get to know them, then it's okay.
- I'm not comfortable with my spouse having opposite sex friends.
- I think you should cut off opposite sex friendships when you get married.

Some individuals are perfectly comfortable with it and some are completely against it. Many are somewhere in between the two extremes. So, what is the correct answer? For me, that depends on the individuals involved and the nature of the friendship. First, I believe that we should have a desire to make our spouse feel comfortable and secure in our marriage so if an opposite sex friendship causes insecurity, adjustments to the friendship may need to be made. Second, most people only consider the possibility of a sexual affair when discussing this topic. I believe that an opposite sex friendship has the ability to rob a marriage of necessary emotional intimacy even if a sexual affair never occurs.

While I do believe that any opposite sex friendship has the potential to become an affair at some point, let's assume that isn't possible and look at three reasons I believe opposite sex friendships can negatively impact a marriage.

1. THEY WILL OFTEN BE AN EASIER PATH TO VALIDATION

Opposite sex friends can often be more attentive and supportive of your dreams and ideas than your spouse will be. Your friend will not be impacted by any of your financial decisions or passion projects so they can provide complete support of any and every idea you ever come up with. Your spouse will be more critical of your thoughts and ideas because it will likely impact them. These factors will make it easier and more rewarding to talk with the friend than your spouse in many situations. There are already enough other relational dynamics in marriage that make it difficult to connect that we don't need an easier option for validation and support.

2. THEY WILL CAUSE UNHEALTHY COMPARISONS

Welcome to the start of every emotional affair: "If my spouse was like you...." Regular conversations and connection with an opposite sex friend can cause comparisons with your spouse: "I wish my spouse laughed at my jokes like they do; I wish my spouse thought my ideas were as great as they do; I wish my spouse was supportive like they are; I wish my spouse understood me the way they do." Comparison is always unfair because we tend to compare the best characteristics of our friend with the worst characteristics of our spouse.

3. THEY WILL STEAL EMOTIONAL INTIMACY FROM YOUR MARRIAGE

Let me explain this idea. If I'm at work all day talking with an opposite sex friend or regularly call an opposite sex friend when I'm commuting and share about my parenting struggles, difficulties with my boss, my dreams of entrepreneurship or just something coming up in my life that I'm excited about, guess what I won't do with my spouse when I get home? You've got it. I don't need to have those conversations with my wife because I have already discussed them with my friend. These conversations will rob my marriage of the emotional intimacy and connection we need to build a strong relationship.

As you can see, finding validation, allowing comparison and outsourcing emotional intimacy can all greatly hurt your marriage, even if you feel like your opposite sex friendship isn't a threat to your relationship. I don't believe that it's impossible to have an opposite sex friend and I don't believe these friendships have to be damaging to the marriage. The key to managing opposite sex friendships in a healthy way will be in how you communicate with your spouse about the friendships and the frequency and depth of conversations you are having. If you manage the frequency, have healthy boundaries about the types and depth of conversations that are occurring and there is clear communication and openness around the friendships, they can be healthy.

TAKE ACTION

Watch
Emotional Affair or Just a Friend?
on the Relationshots *YouTube* channel

1. Discuss with your spouse how you each feel about opposite sex friendships. What are the concerns, if any?

2. Are there any specific opposite sex friendships that make you uncomfortable?

3. Are there any adjustments you would like your spouse to make with their opposite sex friendships?

4. Communicate clearly with each other your expectations around opposite sex friendships so there is no confusion.

5. Which of the three thoughts presented in this chapter have you seen negatively impact your marriage? Discuss your experience with specific examples if possible.

6. What is one adjustment you will make this week to these potential pitfalls and ensure greater connection in the marriage?

CHAPTER 31

THE THREE SIDES OF CONFLICT

Raise your hand if you struggle to manage conflict at times. Conflict is a funny thing because everyone has a different view on conflict. Some people enjoy conflict. Others know it's important and will step into it when needed, though they don't necessarily like it.

Some avoid it at all costs because they dislike tension in their relationships. Others fear conflict because they believe too much conflict will lead to the end of the marriage. No matter what your view of conflict is, know that it is inevitable and even necessary for growth and understanding in marriage.

The reason we often struggle with managing conflict in our relationships is because we aren't aware of all that is going on inside the conflict. No conflict exists in complete isolation by itself. There are actually three sides to every conflict you face: Past, Present and Future. Understanding the three sides of conflict and the three questions you need to be asking will help you successfully manage conflict without causing lasting damage to the marriage.

PAST: WHAT AM I BRINGING WITH ME INTO THIS CONFLICT?

When a conflict arises you won't naturally start thinking about the baggage you may be bringing into the present conflict but it's there. You have baggage from your family of origin, from past relationships, from unresolved issues in the current relationship and from unforgiveness for past hurts in this relationship. All of that can show up immediately in your present conflict.

If you've ever had a fairly innocent conversation go completely sideways, you have experienced the past showing up. Maybe you made a simple suggestion about something you would like your spouse to improve on or do differently and were met with a response like, "I guess I don't do anything right. Maybe you should have married someone else!" Whoa! Slow down there! Pretty sure that wasn't what was communicated. You may not have said or implied that but if your spouse grew up in a home where nothing was ever good enough, where they were criticized for everything they did and where love was given and removed based on performance, you don't have to say much to get that response. The past just showed up in the present conflict!

We all have baggage that we carry into our relationships and if you are not aware of what your baggage is I can guarantee it will negatively influence your conflicts. There are hundreds of scenarios on what this might look like but pay attention to exaggerated responses in conflict and you'll likely uncover some past baggage impacting your present conflict.

PRESENT: WHAT IS THE PRESENT ISSUE AT HAND?

When a conflict occurs it's important to stay focused on the specific issue that has been presented. Before you start evaluating the bigger picture and questioning the stability of the relationship, take a deep breath and respond only to the present issue. What are you actually in conflict about at this moment? Is the conflict about your spouse and a spending issue, picking up after yourself, boundaries with in-laws, parenting, lack of communication or a desire for greater connection? Don't catastrophize the issue. Stay on the specific issue addressed.

The present conflict will also bring into play how you manage and handle conflict as a couple. Are there negative patterns and habits that get triggered? Do immature characters come into play during conflict leading to attack, withdrawal or defensiveness? Is this particular issue resolvable or a perpetual problem? (See Chapter 33 for more on that topic.) The present side of conflict is usually the most obvious and easily addressed but ignoring the past and future sides will hinder your ability to manage the present.

FUTURE: WHAT IS THE GOAL OF THIS CONFLICT?

The answer to this question may seem obvious but there should be some layers to this. The obvious answer would be resolution, right? Everybody wants the conflict resolved so we can move on and reconnect. A future focus should also remind us that there is a bigger picture to the relationship. The goal of your marriage is to remain married until "death do us part." Your goals and vision for the future of the relationship should play a part in how you handle the present side of conflict. Having a vision for your future helps to put the current conflict in perspective. It's likely not as big of a deal as it currently feels.

If you have a future vision for your marriage, you will be less likely to care about getting your way in the current conflict. Your goal shifts from winning the argument to seeking to make sure your spouse feels heard and understood. One of the goals of this present conflict is now about deeper connection and understanding of what your spouse desires in the relationship. Having a future focus will shrink the severity of the current conflict, de-escalating emotions that may be tied to your frustrations. When your present pain becomes greater than your future vision for the relationship, you will want out of the marriage. The presence or lack of a shared future vision for the marriage will either magnify the current conflict or put it into proper focus.

Conflict is a necessary component of relationship and one of the main avenues through which you will learn and understand your spouse. You can't and shouldn't avoid it but you also need to understand how to manage it in a way that doesn't damage the relationship. Successful management of the present issue will require a recognition of the past and future sides as well. Next time you or your spouse bring up an issue in the marriage I encourage you to pause long enough to ask yourselves, "What am I bringing with me into this conflict?" Then remind yourself of the future vision you have for your relationship. Only then will you be able to manage the conflict with clarity.

TAKE ACTION

Watch
3 Sides of Conflict
on the Relationshots *YouTube* channel

1. What baggage do you bring with you into conflicts from your family of origin? *(rejection, abandonment, criticism, performance-based atmosphere, etc.)*

2. What baggage do you bring with you into conflicts from past relationships?

3. What baggage do you bring with you into conflicts from unresolved or unforgiven issues in this relationship?

4. What do you need to do personally to work on or heal this past baggage? What can your spouse do that would help you? (Maybe avoid certain phrases or statements, give more encouragement or praise, etc.)

5. Do you have a future vision for your marriage and what is it? If not, consider a time to sit down together and create one.

6. Commit this week to staying on the present issue when one is brought up and avoid bringing in other issues, past issues or past baggage in justifying or defending yourself. Stay on the present issue, seeking to understand your spouse and resolve their concern.

CHAPTER 32

THREE KEYS TO EMOTIONAL SAFETY

Scientists and psychologists agree that the human species was created for relationship. Relational connections cause us to live longer and experience more happiness and less depression. Emotional isolation, on the other hand, negatively impacts our immune system, making us more susceptible to illness and recovery harder. Our attachment relationships are the primary safe haven for humans and yet many couples struggle to connect emotionally and wouldn't describe their marriage as a safe place.

According to psychologist Sue Johnson who developed Emotionally Focused Couples Therapy, we can evaluate the emotional safety in a relationship by how we answer the following three questions that everybody is unconsciously or consciously asking of their partner. [5]

QUESTION 1: ARE YOU THERE FOR ME?

This question is all about emotional connection. Do you acknowledge the emotional needs of your spouse and are you active in trying to connect with them emotionally? It's easy for couples to settle into a routine where they are just comfortable living together but operating separately. Sadly, disconnection is the norm for many couples.

---
5 Sue Johnson, Hold Me Tight, (New York, NY: Little, Brown and Company, 2008) 47.

Staying connected will require you both to ask and answer this question. The answer to "Are you there for me?" may look different for you and your spouse. You must know your spouse's top emotional needs if you are going to effectively meet their needs on a regular basis. Being "there" for your spouse to listen, support and serve, is key to emotional connection. We all want to know our spouse is there for us and interested in being present with us.

QUESTION 2: DO I MATTER?

Your spouse wants to know their needs matter to you. Conflicts often erupt because one of you feels invisible or invalidated when you try to share and connect. Without actually saying it, couples are wanting the answer to the following questions:

- Do my opinions and ideas matter to you?
- Do you value my perspectives?
- Do I add value to your life?
- Would you miss me if I wasn't around?

Are you aware of the ways your spouse would like you to show them that they are the most important person in your life? What do you practically do to show them you really care about what they have to say. Do you dismiss their ideas and needs or do you demonstrate how their needs are a high priority to you? I'll give you a relevant example of how to get this wrong that occurred twenty minutes ago. While on my phone, I walked into the room where my wife was. I asked her a question and then we started talking. While she was talking I got back on my phone and was looking through some stuff while listening to her. She finally paused and said, "Why are you staring at your phone while I'm talking to you?" Looking at my phone while my wife is talking to me is not a way to show she matters. I got the first part wrong but recovered with my response. Instead of my normal reply, which may have been an excuse or justification, I simply put the phone down and said, "That was rude and I'm sorry."

QUESTION 3: WILL YOU COME WHEN I CALL?

This question is more about physical presence than emotional connection. If your spouse needs you, will you move heaven and earth to get to them? Will you show up physically when they need you most or will you be distracted by and committed to work, hobbies or your family instead? Are you willing to be inconvenienced to show them the relationship matters? Are you so rigid and inflexible with your plans and schedule that pausing or breaking the routine is an annoyance and they know it?

True connection and security in the relationship means we are there for each other even when the other person doesn't ask quite right, is angry, desperate or insecure. Our willingness to show up isn't tied to how we are feeling in the moment or what they have done for us lately. Your spouse desires your undivided attention and full focus, at times, in the relationship. They need to know you'll show up when they call.

Cultivating a safe place in the relationship requires that we ask and then answer these three questions with an emphatic "yes!" Healthy, emotional intimacy is built when couples feel safe and secure. What that "yes" looks like practically will likely be different for you and your spouse so don't assume that your spouse will answer yes simply because you are doing for them what you would want done for you. Discover what a yes looks like for them and be intentional with those things.

TAKE ACTION

Watch
How to Build Emotional Intimacy in Your Relationship
on the Relationshots *YouTube* channel

1. Share with your spouse your current answer to the "Are you there for me?" question. If your answer is "yes" give specific examples of things they do that make you feel like they are there for you. If your answer is "no" give them a few examples of what they could do that would make you feel like they are there for you.

2. Share with your spouse your current answer to the "Do I matter?" question. If your answer is "yes" give specific examples of things they do that makes you feel you matter. If your answer is "no" give them a few examples of what they could do that would make you feel like you matter or how they make you feel like you don't matter.

3. Share with your spouse your current answer to the "Will you come when I call?" question. If your answer is "yes" give specific examples of things they do that make you feel confident they will show up when you need them . If your answer is "no" give them a few examples of what they could do that would make you feel like they will show up when you're in need.

4. Pick one of these three questions that you would like your spouse to put some effort into. Give them two or three things you would like them to begin doing that would lead you to answer the question with a big yes!

CHAPTER 33

RESOLVABLE ISSUES AND PERPETUAL PROBLEMS

Many couples have bought into the myth that there should be some meet-in-the-middle resolution to all of their issues and conflicts and there's probably nothing more exhausting than putting time and energy into trying to resolve an issue that really has no resolution. According to researchers, more than half the problems couples deal with in marriage are actually not resolvable. I want to address the difference between Resolvable Issues and Unresolvable Issues, which are often called "Perpetual Problems," and what to do about each.

Before we jump in, let me remind you that the primary goal of all conflict should be mutual understanding. The goal should not be to win or convince the other person that you're right. The goal isn't even trying to become identical or think the same. Compromise requires that we understand each other's core needs on the issue at hand and that we learn each other's areas of flexibility. Conflict should be a learning experience and we should approach it that way.

Let's look at the two types of conflicts you experience in your relationship. If you don't understand the difference between the two, you will spend unnecessary energy trying to resolve the unresolvable issues leaving you with little or no energy to actually handle the issues that are resolvable.

RESOLVABLE ISSUES

Solvable problems are the situational issues that you deal with day to day. You argue about housework and how to divide responsibilities. You negotiate who is going to pick up the kids from school on Thursdays because it's inconvenient for both of you. You try to make a decision on where to go for vacation and what the budget should be. You attempt to solve the mystery of what to eat for dinner. You go back and forth on line item priorities for the family budget.

These conflicts are about the topic of discussion. There is no deeper meaning behind the position and no childhood wound or personality quirk at the root. It's very specific and situational. He leaves the toilet seat up. She leaves dishes in the sink. He leaves his clothes on the bathroom floor and she somehow gets her hair attached to every piece of laundry he owns. These conflicts are annoying and frustrating but there's nothing deeper behind them. **With solvable problems there is a solution and the solution is sustainable.**

PERPETUAL PROBLEMS (UNRESOLVABLE)

Perpetual problems center on fundamental differences in your personalities or lifestyle preferences. These problems come up over and over again. These could be differences in basic needs, organization, amount of time spent alone or together, how you relate to in-laws or family or punctuality. (Hello, anyone with a "perpetually late" spouse?) You can't solve your personality or preferred lifestyle differences, nor should you try. At the core of managing conflict when it comes to perpetual problems is accepting your partner for who they are. You want to celebrate your differences and learn from each other's differences.

I know you may be thinking, "I can't accept who they are in this specific area because it is detrimental to our relationship." That may be true in some instances where someone is continually unfaithful, has an addiction issue or is abusive. You certainly don't want to accept who they are when it is toxic, abusive or unhealthy. However, that is not the majority of our perpetual problems. Many are not toxic but annoying and frustrating based on what we like or desire, how we think and make decisions or how we prioritize and manage our schedules. As discussed in Chapter 19, Managing Differences, the key to perpetual problems is first to understand our differences and second to accommodate and accept those differences.

TAKE ACTION

Watch
2 Types of Conflict
on the Relationshots *YouTube* channel

1. Make a list together with your spouse of any solvable issues you have argued about lately. Brainstorm possible solutions to these issues while the issue is not heated.

2. Make a list of what you believe are perpetual problems.

3. Pick one perpetual problem each and discuss how you believe your differences in this area cause conflict.

4. Ask your spouse why their position/view/perspective in this area is important to them.

5. Come up with a way you each can celebrate the other's perspective and accommodate them.

6. An example of working through numbers 3-5 might be: The perpetual problem is one person's lack of punctuality. That person asks their punctual partner why it matters to them to be on time. They learn that showing up late represents being disrespectful and not valuing the other's time. They commit to making an effort to be more punctual because they value their partner's desire and perspective.

CHAPTER 34

FIVE MISTAKES WE MAKE WHEN LISTENING

Most people rate themselves as a much better listener than they really are. If you're arguing with me in your head about that fact, you allow me to prove my point. Take just a minute and think through your last five conversations with others. I'm guessing you can recall moments when you either tuned out as the other person was talking, or where you stopped listening and started formulating your response as soon as you heard something that triggered a thought. We all do it. I believe that great communication requires that we become great listeners. In fact, it may be a person's skill at listening rather than talking that determines whether or not they are a good communicator.

We make many mistakes as listeners and often these mistakes are what derail our conversations. Let's look at five common listening mistakes and how you can eliminate these behaviors from your next conversation.

1. DON'T INTERRUPT

I know this seems fairly obvious and definitely isn't really complicated. Most people would agree that interrupting another when they are talking won't elevate your status as a good listener. If you have a tendency to interrupt but don't know why you do it, you probably won't stop interrupting. Is it because you are impatient? Is it because you feel the need to correct what you believe to be a wrong statement? Is it because you think you know where the other person is headed and want to finish it for them? Is it because you don't value their ideas and just want to share your opinion? You will have to identify "why" you interrupt if you want to avoid this listening mistake.

2. DON'T DEFLECT

Deflecting is simply attempting to change the direction of the conversation. When your spouse brings a frustration or grievance to you and you decide to switch subjects or bring in an additional topic, you are deflecting. Some people do this intentionally to avoid taking responsibility or accountability but others do this unconsciously. Listening well will require you to stay on the topic your partner presents.

3. DON'T BLAME

Blaming is really just a counter attack. Your spouse says they would like you to stop talking down to them or criticizing them and you respond with, "You do it to me too." They ask you not to yell at them and you say, "I only yell at you when you attack me." Those responses may be true but aren't effective ways to listen. As you may have learned in Chapter 23 on "Managing the Moment," validation is the only thing that matters at the moment your partner brings an issue to you.

4. DON'T TRY TO PERSUADE

If you don't agree with what is being communicated to you or if you are uncomfortable with where the conversation is going, it can be tempting to try and persuade your partner out of what they are sharing. They share their experience and you respond by telling them how your intention was not to make them feel that way. Your spouse says, "It was really hurtful when you embarrassed me in front of our friends at dinner last night." You respond with, "I wasn't trying to embarrass you. We were all joking around and you were even joking too. Nobody thought any different of you because of that comment." You are trying to convince them not to feel what they are clearly feeling. That's not good listening.

5. DON'T EXCUSE

Nobody likes an excuse no matter how good or valid it sounds. At the end of the day, it's still an excuse. It doesn't matter how tired or hungry you were, how bad your day at work was, how the weather change gave you a headache or how someone called you right after we hung up so you forgot to pick up the prescription. You know the saying, "Excuses are like armpits. Everyone has them and they all stink." Maybe that saying was about opinions but you get the point. Excuses express an unwillingness to take ownership or responsibility. If your spouse brings an issue to you, listen and accept ownership. Don't respond with an excuse.

Your ability to communicate well and resolve conflict in your relationship will depend on your ability to listen well. Avoid these five listening mistakes and you will be well on your way to becoming a great communicator.

TAKE ACTION

Watch
5 Mistakes We Make When Listening
on the Relationshots *YouTube* channel

1. Have your partner rate you on a scale of 1 to 5 in each of the five listening mistakes. *(1 being "needs improvement" and 5 being "area of strength")*

2. Pick the one listening mistake that causes you the most frustration when your partner does it and give an example of how they make this mistake.

3. Tell your partner one thing you plan to do this week to work on your greatest listening mistake.

4. Commit to this action and ask for feedback on how you did one week from today.

CHAPTER 35

THE THREE PHASES OF LOVE

Most people love the idea of "falling in love." The feelings, the obsessive thoughts and the desire for more, motivate a person to often do things they wouldn't normally do, all in the name of love. Movie producers and romance novelists have made a living off selling this idea. The discovery involved in getting to know someone new and the novelty of all the new things experienced together make the process of falling in love so exciting. Can it last? Should it last?

Maybe you've been there or maybe you're there right now. You're not feeling the same way about your spouse as you did in the beginning. You're questioning whether you can get those feelings back. You've "fallen out of love." Does this mean the end of your relationship is imminent or is this just the normal progression of a long term relationship? According to research, you can stay in love if you understand the three phases of love and what is occurring at each stage. Let's take a look at three phases of love according to psychologist and relationship expert Dr. John Gottman. [6]

---

[6] John Gottman, "The 3 Phases of Love," Gottman.com, The Gottman Institute, 2022, https://www.gottman.com/blog/the-3-phases-of-love/.

PHASE 1: FALLING IN LOVE

The process of falling in love is often referred to as "limerence." This phase is highly emotional and feeling-driven. Experts believe this isn't a necessary phase but in the current Western culture of choosing your partner based on romance and passion rather than by an arranged marriage, it is common and expected by most couples. Oddly enough, most arranged marriages even enter into limerence at some point. The "falling in love" phase is highly specific and selective. The person must look right, feel right, smell right and act right to enter limerence.

This phase is represented by phrases such as: "They get me.", "They're the one.", "You complete me." and "God told me you were the person I will marry." Some relationship experts would say that "being in love" can only last 18-24 months but research has shown that it can last indefinitely if all three phases of love are working together.

PHASE 2: TRUST

After falling in love, couples settle into the next phase and begin having some buyers' remorse. All the things that used to attract you to your partner now mildly irritate you. You loved their spontaneity but now their lack of planning and organization cause more frustration than fun. You begin thinking to yourself, "So this is it? I'm going to have to put up with these personality quirks for the next fifty years. I'm going to be having sex for the next five decades with someone who doesn't always see value in taking a shower before bed. People said you don't marry the other persons' family but that clearly isn't true."

Couples usually have the most arguments in the first couple of years of marriage and the majority of these arguments are about trust. Under the surface of many of these conflicts are the following questions about trust:
- Will you be there for me?
- When I'm sad can I count on you?
- If I'm sick will you take care of me? Will I be more important than your mother?

- Will you choose time with me over time with your friends?
- When I need support and encouragement will you provide that for me?
- Will you remain faithful to me?
- On my worst days will you still love me?
- Can I trust you?

This need for building trust is why research continues to show that cohabitating couples are the least stable. Living together without the commitment of marriage equates to saying, "I'm here unless something better comes along or I no longer enjoy this arrangement." When couples are committed to repairing their miscommunications, disappointments, frustrations and moments of conflict, trust is built. This process of navigating and repairing conflict is necessary and healthy in order for couples to build a trusting relationship.

PHASE 3: COMMITMENT

If you were to analyze many of your arguments about family and friendships you'll find they are about loyalty and betrayal at the root. Trust has been built in phase two but now you're really trying to discover whether your partner will remain committed to you no matter what. The questions being asked in this stage are about commitment and loyalty: Am I able to be myself and not worry about your commitment? Can I fall short and struggle without worrying about your faithfulness? Can you see the worst of me and still remain committed? Is your commitment tied to my performance or based on your integrity regardless of how I'm performing?

Research has shown that one of the keys to infidelity is negative comparison. When you start comparing your spouse in a negative light to other options more positively, your commitment will fade. Negative comparison will nurture resentment while cherishing your spouse nurtures greater investment and commitment. Loyalty in long term relationships is tied to gratitude and appreciation. You need to consistently cherish what you have.

So, the question of whether or not you can stay in love is a resounding "yes." Just don't buy into the myth that these feelings of love will just passively stick around allowing you to just do what you feel when you feel like it. That is not mature love. When things are working together in all three phases of love, evidence shows you can stay "in love" for a lifetime. You will need to move past the feeling-driven limerence phase, fight through the trust-building phase and secure yourselves in the commitment phase.

TAKE ACTION

Watch
Can You Stay in Love? The 3 Phases of Love
on the Relationshots *YouTube* channel

1. What are some of the things you experienced in Phase 1: Falling in Love that you would like to do more consistently again? (Regular dates, new experiences, intentional conversations, etc.)

2. Phase 2 is all about trust. Share with your spouse some practical things they do or can do that will strengthen your feelings of trust in the relationship.

3. Share with your spouse some practical things they do that weaken your feelings of trust in the relationship.

4. Take turns answering this question with a true or false. "I am fully confident in your commitment to our relationship." Explain why you answered true or false.

5. What is one thing you desire from your spouse that would strengthen your feelings of trust or commitment in the relationship?

6. Share what you will intentionally commit to do in pursuing your spouse's desire.

CHAPTER 36

THE #1 KEY TO SUCCESS IN MARRIAGE

For a guy who spends the majority of his time working with couples, I'll admit it feels a little weird to identify just one thing as the key to success in marriage. Clearly this book has shown there are many different aspects of a relationship that we must evaluate and manage, so calling something the "#1 key to success" may seem a bit too simple. That said, I still stand by my belief that the presence of authentic community in a couple's life seems to be the number one key to marital success. There are far too many couples who are isolated, who refer to themselves as "private" and don't have other healthy couples who are a part of their marriage. You may be reading this first paragraph and saying to yourself, "No thanks on this whole community stuff. My marriage is my business and I don't need anybody else in it." You may even be able to give me examples of how other people involved in your marriage have actually hurt it more than helped. I would agree with you that anybody and everybody doesn't need to be involved in your relationship, but somebody does.

Having a community for your marriage may be a new concept for you. If you live in a Western culture, marriage is largely a personal decision rather than a family decision. The message we are given around marriage is to find your person and when you do, the rest will take care of itself. If your family and friends don't support your relationship just lean on the love the two of you have and all will work out. Add to this cultural message about marriage a few disappointments and betrayals by family or friends, and you have the perfect recipe for couples to live in isolation from others. You may have a number of friends you spend time with but do they really know what is going on in the difficult moments and struggles of your marriage? If not, you don't have true community.

There are far more than just three reasons for you to consider the importance of community in your marriage but I didn't want to overwhelm you on this one. So, I've decided to focus on three of the more crucial components of community that you should consider. Here are three things community will provide for your marriage that I believe will ensure the success of your relationship.

1. SUPPORT

I know one of the reasons you got married was because your spouse was supportive of your dreams, your goals and your desires in life. I hope that your spouse is your greatest cheerleader in life. I also know that there are moments in every marriage when the person closest to you doesn't feel like your greatest supporter. Frustration, disappointment and hurt will inevitably occur in your marriage. When there is tension and unresolved conflict in your relationship, it is doubtful that you will continue to support at the same level you do when all is good. In those moments and seasons when you just don't like your spouse very much, it will be difficult to cheer them on.

Every marriage will have seasons when we need some outside support to lift us up, encourage us, build us up, push us towards our dreams and fight for our relationship when we feel like giving up. You will experience times in your marriage where you need quality community to provide support and strength because you and your spouse can't seem to get along or get on the same page. Notice that I said, "Quality community." If your community is your girlfriend who is divorced and spends her evenings on dating apps and your single friend who dates married men, they probably won't value the covenant of marriage the way you need your community to do. If your community is your group of guys from college who sleep around or cheat on their wives, you've got the wrong community. You need a community of couples who are focused on building strong marriages.

2. SECURITY

One of the most consistently frustrating things I do is marriage counseling with only one spouse. It is very common to see a client who is seeking to strengthen or repair their marriage by themselves because their spouse is unwilling to get counseling. One of my first questions for this person sitting before me is, "Who has influence in your spouse's life?" I ask this question to determine who might have relational leverage in their spouse's life that we can use to provide accountability. Very rarely can their spouse identify anyone who can hold them accountable. I think the importance of this question is already clear but let me state the obvious. The fact that this person is in counseling by themselves is evidence that their spouse is unwilling to receive accountability from them. If they were accountable, they would be in the counseling office together.

This is why community becomes so important. We will all need outside accountability at times to protect our marriage. My wife's security in our relationship is not her confidence that I will always make the right choices for our marriage (although I'm probably 98.5% on that) but that she has access to men in my life who can hold me accountable when I'm unwilling to allow my wife to do so. Your marriage needs that too! You don't want to be your spouse's only accountability partner because in those seasons where they have decided not to respond to your requests, you will have no other way to influence or call them into account.

3. SANCTIFICATION

I realize this is a big "spiritual" word for Christians that requires a little explaining, so stay with me for a minute. We are all in the process of growing and maturing into who we were created to be. Psychologist Abraham Maslow would call this self-actualization. It is the process of becoming everything you are capable of becoming. For Christians this process is called sanctification.

It is the process of being freed from sin and purified. Whether you want to call this maturing process sanctification or self-actualization, it will require community.

Growth and maturation is often hard and painful. We all have areas of our lives that need healing. It may be wounds from our childhood or past relational pain that is hindering our ability to relate in our marriages in a healthy way. (See Chapter 16 for more on this.) Sometimes our spouse can be a part of this healing and maturation process but other times it is our spouse who continues to trigger those pain points. Even if they mean well, it can feel like rejection and criticism when your spouse points out areas where growth or healing is needed. In those cases you will need outside community to come alongside you and help you to heal and grow. There will be times when you can't see your own issues and will need an outside set of eyes to help you identify problem areas. You will generally be much less sensitive when the person pointing out these things is not your spouse.

Community will give you support when you need it most. Community will provide additional security for your marriage when you or your spouse don't want to be held accountable by one another. Community will be a key component of your personal growth journey. As I conclude this chapter let me clarify one thing as it relates to community. The key to authentic community is the priority and goal of the relationships. You can have lots of couples you spend time with that aren't actually authentic community. The priority of real community is not just to have fun together but to really do life together. There should be a willingness to dig into the difficult areas of your marriages, to hold each other accountable when necessary and to support and encourage each other. You will also have fun times and enjoy moments along the way but the focus is strengthening one another's marriages, not just having fun.

TAKE ACTION

Watch
The #1 Key to Success in Marriage
on the Relationshots *YouTube* channel

1. Would you say that you have authentic community as described in this chapter? If so, identify the couples that are part of that community.

2. Have you ever been hurt by community when you tried to get support or share what was going on in your life?

3. If you do not have community, is this something you are both open to? Discuss why you don't currently have community and what might be preventing you from having it.

FINDING COMMUNITY

If you don't have community or don't even know where to start with developing community, here are a few suggestions:

1. If you are part of a local church community, they often have small groups that meet regularly where you can get connected with other couples.
2. If you have some good friendships with other couples but haven't really shared life at this level, you could identify a few with whom you would like to have authentic community. Share with them what you want to create and ask if they would like to meet regularly (once or twice per month) to support each other's marriages.
3. Our Altared Marriage Membership is a community designed specifically to provide the support, security and sanctification mentioned in this chapter. We would love to be a part of your marriage journey. For more info go to **https://altaredmarriage.com/membership**.

Need community?
Check out the Altared Marriage Membership community.
www.altaredmarriage.com/membership

CHAPTER 37

THE IMPORTANCE OF VALIDATION

There are many things we do to overcomplicate our relationships and honestly, I think a lot of couples struggle relationally because they have too many conflicting messages about relationships coming at them. Unless you jumped straight to this chapter, you have already discovered that I'm pretty simple and practical. This chapter may be one of the more basic concepts in the book but also one of the most important. Validation is a powerful key to intimacy and connection in your marriage. It's not a difficult skill but for many it doesn't come easy and often seems counterintuitive. Validating might be easy when you agree with your spouse's perspective but what about when you don't agree? I'll explain why validation is possible and necessary whether you agree or not.

We all want to feel heard and understood by our partner. Validation is how we make that happen. In Chapter 23 on "Managing the Moment," I discussed how validation can be used effectively to prevent conflict from escalating. Validation is also important when conflict isn't present because it serves as a tool to maintain connection. I believe validation can do three important things for your relationship which is why I want you to develop this simple skill.

1. VALIDATION CREATES CONNECTION

When your spouse shares something with you, their greatest desire in that moment is to be validated. They want to know that you hear them and are seeking to understand them. They usually don't want a solution or an explanation for why their perspective is off, they want connection. Validation provides that connection. When a spouse is seeking connection and they are met with a logical solution in response, they often leave feeling more disconnected. When you feel validated by your spouse you feel connected to your spouse. If you're not sure what validation looks like, consider the following phrases. "I hate that you had to go through that. That sounds painful." "I'm sorry I made you feel that way." "That must have been difficult." "How are you feeling about that?" Any statement or question that expresses empathy and a desire to know more will feel validating to your spouse.

2. VALIDATION PREVENTS ISOLATION

A lack of validation leads to isolation. If you share an experience or your feelings with your spouse but don't feel as though they care and understand you, you will leave the interaction feeling alone. Rather than having a partner by your side, you are stuck navigating these feelings by yourself. Then your spouse turns around and points out some areas where you have messed up and fallen short, leading to more isolation, resentment and anger. Because you didn't feel validated with what you shared, you struggle to then validate what your spouse is sharing and the cycle continues. Invalidation leads to disconnection in the relationship.

3. VALIDATION IS THE PATHWAY TO RESOLUTION

One of the reasons couples struggle with validation is because they believe that agreement is necessary for validation. It seems logical that you would have to agree with your spouse if you are going to validate their perspective but that is not the case. You can validate even when your view of something is different than theirs. You may not agree with their perspective on what occurred but you can still validate them by saying, "I can see why you felt that way based on how you viewed our interaction." You may not agree with what they believed happened or what you feel they said but you can still validate their feelings and perspective. This validation will open up the door for your spouse to be more willing to then hear your perspective. Validation is not an endorsement or even agreement so don't withhold validation because you believe it will cause your spouse to think they are right. As discussed in Chapter 23 on "Managing the Moment", there can be a discussion about what you believe to be the truth at a later time. Validate first, then your spouse will be more receptive to your truth.

Validation is like one of those multi-use tools people keep in their car for emergency situations. It's a screwdriver, hammer, wrench or knife depending on what you need in the moment. Validation can de-escalate a conflict. It can create connection. It can make your spouse feel heard and understood. It can show your partner that you value them. If you can get good at validation your spouse will look forward to conversations with you.

TAKE ACTION

Watch
Why Validation is Vital to Relationships
on the Relationshots *YouTube* channel

1. Ask your spouse how they would rank you on the skill of validation on a scale of 1 to 5. *(1 being "needs improvement" and 5 being "area of strength".)*

2. Give your spouse an example of something they do or could do that will feel validating to you.

3. Give your spouse an example of something they do that feels invalidating to you. *(e.g. minimizing, excusing or explaining away things)*

4. Commit to validating your spouse this week when they share something with you and evaluate how that changed your interactions at the end of the week.

CHAPTER 38

THREE CONNECTION KILLERS

Relational satisfaction will always be tied to feelings of connection. When you feel connected to your spouse you will see them and the relationship in a positive light. When you feel disconnected you will struggle to extend grace, forgive and believe the best about your spouse. Maintaining a healthy connection in marriage will require you to consistently and intentionally implement behaviors that help the relationship grow while removing things that cause division and disconnection. If you want to stay connected in your marriage, it's important for you and your spouse to be aware of the things that cause each of you to feel disconnected. Some of these things will be specific to the two of you and easy to spot based on your personalities, top emotional needs and love languages, but there are some subtle things that can creep into any relationship and damage the connection. Let's take a look at three common connection killers that will likely show up in your relationship.

1. CHILDREN

Before you get offended on behalf of your children let me explain. I'm not criticizing your children or implying that children are a bad thing. I'm simply suggesting that if you have children, they will absolutely impact the connection you have with your spouse. Children demand your attention. Children require the expenditure of time and energy. Children impact your finances. Children will expose areas of weakness in your character. Children will cause division in your marriage as they attempt to play mom and dad against each other to get their way.

It is easy for children to become so consuming that your marriage takes a back seat. A good number of couples become disconnected during the child rearing years and struggle to regain that connection once the children grow up and move out. Yes, your children will move out one day or at least, should move out. That might be a discussion for a different chapter or book, but for now let's assume a healthy parenting model where children grow up, become adults and develop emotional, relational and financial independence. Your spouse isn't going anywhere so make sure to schedule times of "children-free" connection with your spouse on a regular basis.

2. CALENDAR

If I asked you to pull out your calendar right now and tell me what is on there, you would be the norm rather than the exception if you told me there is nothing on your calendar related to time with your spouse. For most couples the calendar gets filled with work requirements, children's activities, necessary appointments, hobbies and family commitments, leaving little or no time for connection in the marriage. The belief is that times of connection will just naturally and organically occur as we go about life together. This is rarely the case.

Couples that stay connected are couples that make their calendars work for them rather than allowing their calendars to dictate their lives. The next chapter is dedicated to helping you intentionally use your calendar to create consistent moments of connection in your marriage so we'll continue this discussion in the pages to follow.

3. COMPARISON

There may be nothing that can quickly make you feel bad about your relationship like seeing someone else's relationship that appears to be better than what you are experiencing. Have you ever had that happen? You're minding your own business, feeling pretty good about your life, and then see someone's social media post about how great their spouse is and how amazing their relationship is. Now you're second guessing your marriage, feeling shortchanged and wondering if there is something better out there for you. What in the world just happened? Comparison just snuck up on you.

The problem with comparison is that we usually compare others' best moments with our worst moments. We're comparing the fantasy of what others choose to put forth with the reality of what we are currently experiencing. I'll let you in on a little secret. Having counseled couples for more than a decade, it has been my experience that the couples who post the most about how amazing their spouse is and how blessed and lucky they are to be married to this amazing person, are the same couples who were sitting in my office two days prior talking about how they're ready to end the relationship. Don't believe the hype. Comparison will kill your connection by causing discontent and resentment. Spend your energy on things that will strengthen intimacy and connection with your spouse rather than speculation about what relationship would be like with someone else.

Children, comparison and a busy calendar will fight against connection in your relationship. Sadly, they often sneak up on you before you even know what's happened. The good news is you are in complete control of all three and can guard your relationship against their negative impact on your marriage.

TAKE ACTION

Watch
Top 3 Marriage Killers
on the Relationshots *YouTube* channel

1. If you have children, identify some of the ways you feel they cause disconnection in your marriage. What are some things you can do to prevent this?

2. Take a look at your calendars and count how many activities you have scheduled for your marriage and how many you have for other things. Talk about what you would like to see on your calendar to strengthen your marriage.

3. Is negative comparison something you struggle with in your relationship? What specific aspects of your relationship do you most often compare because you desire improvement or growth?

4. What is one change that you would like to see in your marriage that would minimize or eliminate one of the three connection killers mentioned in this chapter?

5. Commit this week to implement the changes that you each identified in the previous question and evaluate the impact this had at the end of the week.

CHAPTER 39

THE BUSINESS OF MARRIAGE

If you are the planner, list maker and scheduler in your relationship then you are going to love this chapter. In fact, you may have looked at the table of contents and come straight to this chapter first. If you're the hopeless romantic who believes that relational chemistry and spontaneity are the keys to a thriving marriage...well, you probably put this book down and picked up a Nicholas Sparks novel a long time ago anyway. There are some things in life that we can choose to ignore or deny and still face the consequences but they are a reality. We may want to pretend that things like gravity, taxes, death and middle-aged mothers on TikTok don't exist but they still do. Let me add one more to that list. Your marriage has a business side to it. I know that doesn't sound very romantic but the sooner you understand this the better you'll be able to enjoy the relational side of your marriage.

I think it's safe to say that nobody started the dating process looking to find that perfect someone with whom they could pay the bills, disagree on parenting strategies and argue about the finances. Most people choose to get married because they really enjoy spending time with the other person. They enjoy losing track of time on the phone chatting about nothing. They look forward to special date nights at a new restaurant. They long for a warm embrace after extended time apart. Then something strange happens. Two people get married, get busy with life and suddenly find themselves distant, disconnected and wondering if they married the wrong person. Nope. There's nothing wrong with the person you chose. You simply failed to understand that marriage has both a relational and business side to it.

In every marriage there is both a business component and a relational component. You and I got married for the fun, relational aspect of marriage. The dating process sets us up for disappointment in marriage by only highlighting the relational side while feeding the lie that a business approach has no place in the relationship. Many couples get a few years into marriage, add some financial responsibilities, a dog, a couple of kids and soon feel like every interaction has become a "business" conversation. Did you pay the mortgage? Can you take Kendal to the dentist on Tuesday? The washing machine is leaking. We need to purchase tickets to see my family this summer. Amy's teacher emailed to let us know she hasn't turned in her homework this week.

At this point couples get nervous and believe something is wrong with the marriage. This is where the old cliché, "I love him but I'm not in love with him" enters the conversation. There is absolutely nothing wrong with you, your spouse or the marriage. The problem is that you are still operating with a faulty mindset you developed through movies and romance novels and fueled through the dating process. You don't need a new spouse, you only need a simple shift in mindset. The key to enjoying your relationship is not to wish away or avoid the business side of the marriage, it's to make sure you are keeping the business part of marriage and the relational part of marriage distinct and separate from one another. If you don't intentionally separate the two sides of marriage, the business side will always take over and consume the fun, relational side.

I want to propose that you and your spouse implement three specific interactions each week to ensure the business side of marriage is taken care of while making sure you also get to enjoy the fun, relational side of your marriage.

1. STAFF MEETING

I suggest that you schedule one staff meeting each week to make sure the business side of marriage is addressed regularly and systematically. This is a time to discuss family logistics (appointments, travel, goals and tasks, etc.), budgets, and to ask each other for feedback on any areas of the relationship you've identified for growth or adjustment. Having a specific time to discuss the business side of marriage will free up other times throughout the week from the burden of these types of conversations.

The planner in your relationship will value these staff meetings because they can't relax and have fun if the business has not been handled. The one who normally avoids these conversations will be glad to have them designated at a specific time so they aren't taking over all conversations throughout the week. Set yourselves up for success by knowing when enough is enough. Don't schedule an hour long staff meeting if you know that you or your spouse will start checking out at the thirty minute mark. You may need to keep the staff meeting short and consider doing two each week if one longer staff meeting isn't successful. I would suggest start with just one and keep it fairly short until you get comfortable with it and find what seems to work for you both.

2. DATE NIGHT

Just as you designate a specific day and time for your staff meeting, pick a day and time for date night. This is a time for connection without distraction. It doesn't always have to be outside the house if finances or childcare are a struggle. It could be as simple as some popcorn, snacks and a movie together after the kids have gone to bed. The key to date night is to avoid any and all "business" conversations. Don't make a reservation at your favorite restaurant, get dressed up, sit down for dinner and start talking about the kids and upcoming week. If you struggle avoiding these conversations just download some couples' questions off the internet and spend the evening asking and answering questions designed to connect you. The goal is to enjoy time together. Logistical discussions, problem solving and conflict-resolving conversations are off limits on date night.

3. QUICK CONNECTIONS

Quick connections are short moments of interaction focused on staying emotionally and relationally connected. These can be as short as 10-15 minutes long. You might share your high and low for the day. It may be a devotional or prayer together for people of faith. You could play a game together or take turns giving foot or back rubs while talking about the day. The goal is connection so avoid activities or discussion topics that may lead to conflict. I suggest at least two quick connections each week because I believe couples need to have more relational conversations each week than business conversations to create a marriage where both feel connected, cared for and loved.

If you're keeping track, that's one staff meeting, one date night and two quick connections each week. If you're thinking you don't have time for all of that, I'm here to say you can't afford not to make time for these moments. It will only require two hours of your week to have a thirty minute staff meeting, one hour date night and two separate fifteen minute quick connections. You will be amazed at what these intentional times can do for your marriage. You will prevent the business side of the relationship from taking over while ensuring times of fun and enjoyment together that may have been missing for quite some time.

TAKE ACTION

Watch
Why Your Marriage Is an Essential Business
on the Relationshots *YouTube* channel

1. What do you like or dislike about the idea of a weekly staff meeting? How long would you want the staff meeting to be?

2. What are some things you would like to do for a date night?

3. What are some activities that you would like to do for the quick connections?

4. Get out your calendar and schedule the staff meeting, date night and two quick connections each week for the next month. If travel prevents you from being together you can still create these moments by phone or video call.

It will likely take some practice and adjustments to find a rhythm that works well for you so don't give up if the staff meeting, date night or quick connections don't feel successful the first few times you do them. Stay committed and stay consistent and you will find what works best for your relationship.

CHAPTER 40
FIVE REASONS TO COMBINE YOUR FINANCES

Finances usually tops the list of things couples argue most about because so many things are tied to money. People's security, fears, image, self-control, future, dreams, identity and much more are represented in how they view and handle their finances. Money is important and for many it's highly personal. Mess with people's money and you'll see what they are really like! It used to be a given that couples who married would combine their finances and manage it together but I have found that the rise of second marriages and the prevalence of people waiting longer to get married have complicated financial arrangements in marriage.

Many couples are deciding to keep finances separate and split household bills rather than to share a joint account and manage their money together. I won't take the time here to dissect the many reasons for this arrangement but often times it is driven by fear, lack of trust or past experiences and hurts. I know some couples that seem to effectively manage their finances this way and can do so without damaging the relationship but for the majority of couples it will usually create more conflict and division. For this reason, I would like to give you five reasons you should consider combining finances in marriage.

1. TRANSPARENCY BUILDS INTIMACY

I'm guessing you desire a close, intimate relationship with your spouse. Transparency in all areas of the relationship will be vital to maintain that closeness and connection. A lack of information or the withholding of information in the area of finances will hurt your ability to strengthen the connection with your spouse. When there is a lack of communication and an absence of information, people begin to create their own narratives and fill the gaps in information with suspicion and mistrust. Full transparency in your finances will strengthen intimacy.

2. SEPARATENESS LEADS TO MORE SEPARATENESS

When it comes to any area of your relationship, what you feed will grow. If your finances are separate then you will likely stop having financial conversations and making joint financial decisions. This will make it easier to also avoid conversations in other areas of the relationship and making independent decisions can become the norm.

3. THERE'S NO "I" IN "WE"

You've heard all the cliché sayings before: "There's no "I" in team. Teamwork makes the dream work." You get the point. The goal of marriage is oneness in all areas of the relationship. Separate financial accounts will lead to a "me and you" mentality rather than a "we" focus. If you split the bills and both spouses are always able to cover their part, there won't be any problems. The moment one spouse comes up short on their responsibilities either due to poor management or some unforeseen circumstance, will be an opportunity for "me versus you" to come into play.

Your inability to cover your bills now becomes your spouse's problem as well. They will feel that it's unfair for them to sacrifice in order to cover your responsibility and resentment will kick in. After a few of those uncomfortable and critical conversations in the marriage you both will soon stop sharing where you are at financially with each other. You can see where this is headed and why communication and oneness are so important.

4. ALLOWS FOR ACCOUNTABILITY

One aspect of a healthy marriage is the accountability each spouse provides for the other. We all need accountability in our relationships, our decision-making, our priorities, our time management and more. If your spouse has no involvement in your finances they won't be able to hold you accountable for your individual and shared goals. You can't hold someone accountable for what you can't see or access. If your spouse doesn't want you to have access to their finances it should bring up another question: Why don't they want accountability?

5. ELIMINATES INCOME DISPARITIES

In most marriages there is a difference in income between the two people. One of you may work while the other manages the family or you both work but have different incomes. If your goal is oneness it doesn't make sense for one of you to be struggling while the other has a lot of financial margin. This can begin to create a power imbalance in the marriage where the higher income earner believes they should have more input, be able to make the final call on decisions or even distribute and withhold money in the relationship as a control mechanism. If the money is combined and clearly belongs to both of you, you will eliminate any actual or perceived disparities in the relationship.

I realize some couples have found a system that works for them where finances are kept separate but you are definitely the exception if this is your model. For the majority of couples who choose not to combine their finances, the result is more potential for secrecy and division. If this is a new concept for you and there is fear around giving up full control of your money, I would suggest beginning with an honest conversation about your fears. Share why this will be hard for you and pick a simple step to begin moving towards fully combined finances. Maybe you open a joint account and agree to put a certain amount in together as a way to get started and build trust. Maybe you start with a weekly or twice monthly finance meeting where you start the dialogue around money and budgets, getting comfortable with talking about money before actually starting to combine your money. Start the conversation and begin working towards greater transparency and trust in this area.

TAKE ACTION

Watch
Should Couples Combine Their Bank Accounts or Keep Them Separate?
on the Relationshots *YouTube* channel

1. If you currently don't combine your finances, why have you picked this approach? What would be your fears in combining your finances?

2. If you already combine your finances, are you happy with the current setup and how you communicate about your finances? If not, what would you like to see change?

3. Would you like to have your spouse be more involved in the finances? What specifically do you want that to look like?

4. If you don't already have one, develop a plan for regular conversations about your finances to create more transparency in your relationship.

CHAPTER 41

FIVE REASONS COUPLES STOP SHARING WITH EACH OTHER

It's very difficult to fix something that's broken if you don't know why it isn't working. A lot of couples who come in for counseling know they've grown apart and are clear their communication is lacking but don't often know why this has happened. They feel the same way I do when taking my car to the mechanic. "It's making a weird noise when I accelerate and it just doesn't drive like it used to but I'm not sure where the issue is coming from." If your communication is not where you would like it to be, evaluate the following five reasons many couples struggle to share with each other. If your communication is great, then make a mental note of these five categories so you can avoid future disconnection in your relationship.

1. PAST FEARS

We've already determined that everyone comes into marriage with relational pain and baggage (See Chapter 16). If you or your spouse learned from past experience that sharing and opening up usually lead to bad outcomes like rejection, verbal abuse, anger, disapproval, attack, criticism, judgment or withdrawal, you will be fearful about sharing concerns or desires. Past fears around sharing can cause a person to prefer no communication and peace over the possibility of tension and conflict. You may be able to avoid the things you fear most but intimacy will suffer as a result.

2. INABILITY

You may have grown up in a family where good communication wasn't modeled or taught. If that's the case, it's likely that communication in the beginning of your relationship was easy because the content shared generally lacked depth and vulnerability. But as a relationship deepens and attachment grows so does the necessity for skills to navigate conversations at this level. An inability to connect on a deeper emotional level prevents many couples from sharing, especially when something severe occurs in the relationship such as financial ruin or the loss of a loved one. The issue and pain are so great there can be an inability to communicate about it.

3. LACK OF SAFETY

One of the necessary ingredients for open sharing is the feeling of safety. Your spouse must feel that you are a safe space if they are going to risk transparency and vulnerability. If your partner shares feelings or frustrations with you and is met with defensiveness, blame, judgment or attack, they will quickly decide your relationship is not safe. Instead of choosing to share and connect they will remain silent.

4. SHAME

Personal shame will cause many people to shrink back from sharing. Many times, an addiction, embarrassing moment or habitual struggle will lead someone to believe they will risk losing their partner's love if they expose this area of themselves. Shame will cause you to believe another person won't accept you if you can't even accept this part of you. Shame will keep your heart on lockdown, hiding some areas of your life from everyone around you. If you believe that sharing your deepest struggles or greatest failures will result in rejection, you'll never open up to your spouse in ways that leave you feeling vulnerable.

5. INSECURITY

When it comes to baggage from past relationships or our family of origin, insecurity often sits at the top of the list. Maybe you grew up in a family where your opinions and requests were ignored or minimized. Maybe partners in past relationships made you feel that the expression of your desires and needs was selfish and put unfair pressure on others. It may even be that you've realized from experience that your desires aren't going to be fulfilled anyway so there's no point in expressing them. Negative past experiences around sharing can cause a person to believe their desires and wants are unimportant and they shouldn't bother anyone else with these needs.

As you can see there are many reasons people shut down and stop sharing with each other leading to disconnection and isolation in the relationship. Intimacy requires regular and honest communication. Withholding your true feelings or desires is not selflessness but dishonest and will ultimately hurt the relationship. I encourage you to develop the habit of evaluating what is really going on any time you find yourself hesitating to open up and share with your spouse. Identify what is preventing your willingness to be vulnerable and share that awareness so you can create an environment in the relationship that promotes transparency and healthy communication.

TAKE ACTION

Watch
Why Couples Stop Sharing With Each Other
on the Relationshots *YouTube* channel

1. Identify which of the five areas you believe prevent you from sharing at times. Where did this concern come from? *(past relationships, childhood, current relationship, etc.)*

2. Are there things your spouse does currently that reinforce your reason for not sharing?

3. What is something you would like your spouse to stop doing that would make your relationship feel like a safer place to share?

4. What is something your spouse can do that would help you to share and open up more?

5. Identify one thing that you will each work on to create a relationship where sharing and vulnerability are welcome and cherished.

CHAPTER 42
THE POWER OF APPRECIATION

You already know that I believe the simple things done consistently make all the difference in relationships. There may not be any relationship skill that's as easy to understand and execute as appreciation. You likely learned it as a kid when adults regularly asked you the question, "What do you say?" after someone gave you something, attempting to teach you the value of saying "thank you." Appreciation may feel like too simple an action to make much of a difference but I can promise you that amazing things happen in a relationship where appreciation is expressed.

According to research, people who receive regular appreciation at work are five times more engaged and productive. Sadly, the average ratio of positive to negative feedback in the workplace is 1:10. Studies of families indicate the norm at home is 1:14 with our children. And we wonder why our children tend to be negative and defensive. Experts suggest that successful, long-term relationships need an average of 5:1 positive to negative interactions. I'm guessing that's an area you could improve.[7] Let's talk about what that looks like and what often prevents us from showing more appreciation in our relationships. Here are three reasons we struggle with appreciation.

---

7   Kyle Benson, "The Magic Relationship Ratio, According to Science." Gottman.com, Gottman Institute, 2022, https://www.gottman.

1. TOO FOCUSED ON WHERE WE WANT TO BE

Goals are great and looking to the future is important. It's also true that a future focus will keep your eyes on what's ahead and prevent you from appreciating where you are and how far you have come.

2. TOO FOCUSED ON WHAT'S MISSING

I'm not against regular evaluation of your relationship to see where you both need to change and grow. That's one of the goals of a staff meeting. (See Chapter 39) However, too much focus on what still needs to change or what you believe is missing in the relationship will leave you feeling discontent. It's hard to be appreciative of your spouse when you are focused on what they still aren't doing. Appreciation allows us to focus on the growth and not just the gap between where we are and where we want to be.

3. SPOUSE DOESN'T RECEIVE APPRECIATION WELL

Some people don't receive compliments or appreciation well, e.g. You receive a compliment and downplay with some self-deprecating humor or dismiss it altogether. If this occurs often the other person in the relationship will eventually stop showing appreciation. If that's you, just say, "You're welcome" or "Thank you" depending on the nature of the compliment and then shut up. Nothing else is needed.

Living in the here and now makes appreciation possible. If you tend to be a goal setter and are a results-driven person, you will need to slow down at times in order to appreciate what you have and where you have grown as a couple. You may even need to schedule some time into each day to pause for a minute and think through all that you appreciate about your relationship. I think appreciation is pretty simple and may be second nature to you, but if it isn't, here are four quick tips to increase appreciation in your relationship.

1. Look for it

I told you it was simple. We don't usually notice things we're not looking for. We even have a little part of our brain whose job it is to notice the things we've determined are important. I won't take the time to explain it all now but if you've ever decided to shop for a new car and suddenly begin seeing the type of car you are shopping for everywhere, then you have experienced the "Reticular Activating System" at work. This group of neurons at the base of your head near the spinal cord is tasked with filtering incoming stimuli and determining what is worth noticing. If you are looking for things to appreciate, you will see them.

2. See it and say it

When you see something that you can appreciate, don't wait. Express it right then and right there. It is easy to think of something you appreciate and then decide you are going to share it with your spouse later on when you see them or have time to talk. Do it in the moment so you don't forget. If you're at work and think of something, stop for thirty seconds and text your partner. When you sit down for a dinner you didn't cook, appreciate the one who did cook. If you put on a shirt you didn't wash, thank the one who laundered your clothes. When you realize there is a new trash bag in the kitchen, thank the person who took out the trash. Say it as soon as you see it.

3. Be specific

"I appreciate you," is a nice general statement and most people would be happy to hear that. Expressing specific appreciation is even better. When you express appreciation, you can do it in two specific areas, the person or the performance. Performance appreciation might sound like, "I appreciate you filling my car up with gas." "I appreciate you listening to me without being distracted by your phone." There's a saying that what gets celebrated gets repeated so appreciation is a great way to get more of what you like. You can also appreciate your spouse for who they are and not just their specific performance. "I appreciate how positive you always are." "You are a great friend. Your friends are lucky to have you in their lives." Specific appreciation feels more personal than general and will show your spouse that you notice their efforts.

4. Journal it

Many people promote keeping a gratitude journal as a good way to stay focused on the good things in your life. I want to encourage you to keep an appreciation journal on the things you appreciate about your spouse so you can read it regularly as a reminder of how great they are. Our natural tendency is to focus in on the negative since these are things causing us frustration and pain. An appreciation journal will help combat this tendency and allow us to avoid the negative comparisons that lead to discontentment in a relationship.

Appreciation really is the "secret sauce" to keeping love alive and well in a relationship. You can't overdo appreciation but its absence will create an atmosphere where the more difficult discussions necessary in marriage won't find success. Remember, your relationship needs a 5:1 ratio of positive to negative interactions to thrive. A lack of appreciation will make it almost impossible to give critical feedback or have hard conversations. Appreciation softens the environment and lowers defensive walls making the path to resolving conflict smooth.

TAKE ACTION

Watch
The Power of Appreciation in Relationships
on the Relationshots *YouTube* channel

1. How would you rate yourself in giving appreciation on a scale of 1 to 5? *(1 is needs improvement and 5 is area of strength)* Does your partner agree with you?

2. Which of the three reasons people struggle to appreciate do you identify with most?

3. What is one thing you can do to fight against this struggle?

4. Practice the art of appreciation right now by telling your spouse one thing you appreciate about who they are or something they have done.

5. Commit this week to expressing appreciation to your spouse at least once per day and then share with each other how this felt once the week has ended. Next week commit to appreciation twice per day.

CHAPTER 43

WHAT'S ACCEPTABLE SEXUALLY IN MARRIAGE?

I'm not sure if you grew up in a home where sex was talked about regularly or talked about rarely. I'm not sure if you have a church community or group of friends where sex is talked about. I'm not sure if you and your spouse talk about sex. What I do know is that many couples have questions about sex and often have a hard time finding safe places for honest dialogue around sexual activity in marriage. I won't be able to address every question you have about sex in this chapter but I do want to have a discussion around four specific areas of sexual activity. Many couples wonder if porn, toys, oral sex and anal sex are acceptable activities in marriage. Some are asking from a biblical point of view and others from a secular point of view. I will give you my thoughts on these four areas from both a biblical and secular worldview.

Let's go with a biblical worldview first. If you are a Christian your thoughts, attitudes and behaviors should be informed biblically. When the Bible speaks on a subject or principle you should desire to line up with that view because you know that God's desire for you is to live in freedom rather than bondage. God's principles are designed to allow the Christian to live in complete freedom, not to burden them with a set of rules aimed at behavioral control.

BIBLICAL

Philippians 2:3-4 says, "Do nothing from selfishness or empty conceit, but with humility consider one another as more important than yourselves; do not merely look out for your own personal interests, but also for the interests of others." If your focus in the area of your sexual relationship is You and what You want, you are already approaching this conversation from the wrong place. The foundational principle for a biblical discussion of sexual activity should be selflessness rather than selfishness.

ORAL SEX

The Bible does not condemn or speak against oral sex specifically but does seem to suggest in the book of Song of Solomon that there's nothing wrong with it. In chapter two the wife is talking and says, "I delight to sit in his shade and his fruit is sweet to my taste."(Song of Solomon 2:3) In Song of Solomon, chapter four, the woman responds to the man's description of her and mentions him coming into "her garden" and "tasting its choice fruits."(Song of Solomon 4:16) These verses and others like them may seem to suggest oral pleasure in the relationship. This may be more metaphor than literal description, but the Bible does not say oral sex is sin, so it would be acceptable if both spouses are comfortable with it.

ANAL SEX

The Bible does not address anal sex between husband and wife, so if someone is saying that anal sex is "sodomy" and the Old Testament talks about the sin of Sodom, they are taking those specific passages beyond their original meaning. The story of Sodom was about homosexual sex between men and the town was condemned for a number of sexual sins. We'll discuss anal sex more in the secular worldview section below but the Bible does not specifically address anal sex between husband and wife.

PORNOGRAPHY

Let's take a look at two scriptures in addressing pornography in marriage. Hebrews 13:4 says, "Marriage should be honored by all, and the marriage bed kept pure, for God will judge the adulterer and all the sexually immoral." Some would consider viewing pornography as bringing a third party into the marriage bed, although digitally and may constitute adultery. That might be a stretch but bringing these sexual images into your minds as you are engaging sexually with your spouse would not be keeping the "marriage bed pure."

In Matthew 5:28 Jesus says, "But I tell you that anyone who looks at a woman lustfully has already committed adultery with her in his heart." Now, I'm not here for a theological debate about this area of scripture being intentional exaggeration and hyperbole by Jesus to make a point rather than literal proclamations. The very next verse tells a person to pluck out their eye and throw it away if it causes them to stumble. I'm guessing Jesus didn't really want people to gouge out their eyes. Jesus is suggesting that our thoughts and heart intentions are equally as important as physical actions, so lusting after a person through the viewing of pornography is akin to adultery in our hearts. Lusting after another would also break the 10th commandment of coveting our neighbor's wife. Biblically, I believe it's pretty clear that pornography is not acceptable nor helpful to your marriage.

TOYS

The Bible doesn't address sex toys so there's nothing here to discuss biblically. Let's now shift from a biblical to secular worldview and review the acceptability of pornography, toys, oral sex and anal sex in marriage.

SECULAR

The shift from a biblical to secular worldview when approaching sex in marriage requires us to shift from asking the question "Is it sin?" to the question "Is it wise?" Does the introduction of something sexually into your marriage have the potential to do more harm than good? A healthy sexual relationship is one in which neither spouse is feeling pressured or forced to do something they don't want to do sexually. Neither person should feel shame or resentment from engaging in something sexually with their spouse. Much like the biblical approach, sexual intimacy should not be about selfishness.

ORAL SEX

If your spouse is good with giving or receiving oral sex and there are no hygiene issues that would make it unsafe or unwise, go for it! Many people are uncomfortable with oral sex because they worry about smells or tastes. If your spouse is uncomfortable with oral sex have an honest conversation about why this is and see if there are some things you both can do to alleviate the concerns. Again, the goal is not to coerce or pressure your spouse into something they don't want to do but to eliminate concerns if there is a desire but fear around giving or receiving oral sex.

ANAL SEX

Since we're not looking at anal sex from a moral perspective, what should be considered when determining if it is acceptable or not in marriage? I think we appeal to wisdom and logic. Logic would tell us that the natural function of the rectum was not for sexual penetration. The rectum is not self-lubricating like the vagina and the tissues that make up its walls are thinner than the vagina so there is a higher likelihood of them tearing. It's also true that feces carry bacteria so tears in the wall can get infected. Additionally, if couples are moving from anal to oral or vaginal sex, they can transport bacteria into the mouth or vagina. Logic says that the body was not naturally created for anal sex and wisdom would say if couples decide to engage in anal sex there needs to be a lot of discussion, planning and care taken to make sure harm is not being done.

PORNOGRAPHY

The secular approach to pornography dismisses any moral concerns around it and instead simply asks the question, "Is bringing porn into your marriage wise?" Let me give you a couple of things to consider when deciding whether or not to bring pornography into your sexual relationship in marriage.

Comparison: Viewing pornography can cause comparison in your sexual relationship. Pornography is not real and yes, they are actors so this can lead to disappointment or frustration with the real sex in your relationship. Unrealistic and unhealthy expectations are damaging in any aspect of your relationship. Your sexual intimacy can be damaged by unrealistic comparisons and expectations.

Psychological Impact: Pornography can be addicting for many physiological and psychological reasons we don't have time to fully develop and discuss right now. Introducing pornography into your marriage can possibly lead to one or both of you becoming addicted. Research has shown that viewing pornography can release more dopamine in the brain, because of its "novelty," than sex with a familiar partner. This dopamine rush that you get from viewing new images can cause you to become less satisfied with familiar, real-life sex partners (aka your spouse).

Those two thoughts to consider are just barely scratching the surface of many different ways pornography can negatively impact your sexual intimacy. Volumes of books have been written on the dangers of pornography so I would encourage you to read and research more if you feel that viewing pornography together is good for your marriage. Wisdom would suggest that pornography is not beneficial for your marriage and can be very detrimental.

TOYS

Toys seem to be the most neutral category in our discussion, so let me just give you a couple of things to consider when trying to decide if they should be a part of your marriage. Answer the following questions for yourself.

Could the use of toys with your spouse lead to you deciding to use them in place of your spouse? I'm not going to take the time to run down the road of masturbation but if the relationship has conflict or tension it will be easier to use the toys yourself instead of engaging with your spouse, which can ultimately cause disconnection in the marriage. It might be wise to set some rules around the use of toys so they don't become a substitute for sexual intimacy between the two of you.

If you get used to what the toys can do, will regular sex with your spouse become less satisfying or unsatisfying? Your husband's hands, mouth and genitals can't move at the speed of a vibrator. Your husband's penis cannot remain hard indefinitely like a dildo. Toys can do things the human body can't, which is why they can be helpful in pleasuring and reaching orgasm during sex. It also means they could ultimately make natural sex with your spouse unsatisfying or unenjoyable.

    Hopefully, this chapter has challenged you to think through these four areas of sexual activity in your marriage. You likely have other questions since there is no end to variety and approaches when it comes to sexual intimacy in marriage. I'm guessing the guiding principles we used to approach these four areas will also apply to any other topic you want to address. Use wisdom and selflessness as your foundation and the questions will likely help answer themselves.

TAKE ACTION

Watch
Oral, Anal, Porn & Toys... What's Sexually Acceptable in Marriage?
on the Relationshots *YouTube* channel

1. Are there any of the four areas discussed in this chapter that you desire to do with your spouse?

2. Are there any of the four areas that you are completely against? If so, why?

3. Do you feel pressured by your spouse to do things sexually that make you uncomfortable? Discuss why you are uncomfortable and what if anything might allow you to be open in this area.

4. What other areas of your sexual relationship would you like to discuss? You're already talking about a difficult subject so might as well keep going now!

5. What is one thing you can commit to doing for each other that will keep your sexual intimacy a priority?

6. What is one thing your spouse could do that would help you to feel more comfortable and safe in your sexual relationship?

CHAPTER 44

FIVE STEPS TO REPAIRING AFTER CONFLICT

Conflict is inevitable in your relationship; trying to avoid conflict is a terrible relationship strategy. I'm a natural conflict avoider so trust me on this one. I like peace. Peace isn't necessarily bad but the absence of conflict by itself is not necessarily an indicator of a great relationship. If you believe conflict is always bad you will likely find yourself both frustrated and disappointed in your relationship. You will be pursuing a reality that doesn't exist while avoiding some important conversations necessary for your relationship.

The key to conflict is not avoiding it at all costs but rather how you recover and repair after conflict. Couples who report being happy and satisfied in their marriages are couples who handle their conflicts in gentle and positive ways. They are couples who listen to one another's perspectives, seek to understand each other and work together to find a compromise that works for both. (See Chapter 24 on How to Compromise for more ideas on that topic.) That last sentence may sound like some far-off dream or romantic comedy script compared to your current reality. If you're like me, there are times when you don't handle conflict well; like when you say some things you wish you could take back and when you hurt one another. That happens to the best of us. Repairing the relationship then becomes the priority. As you seek to repair after conflict consider these five steps to guide your process.

STEP 1: EXPRESS YOUR FEELINGS

Each of you take turns talking about how you were feeling during the conflict. Were you feeling sad, angry, worried, defensive, unappreciated, disrespected, defensive or out of control? Share whatever emotion was being experienced in that moment. The only emotion we usually see expressed by our spouse in an argument is anger so this step will help you both really understand what was going on in the other person.

STEP 2: SHARE YOUR PERSPECTIVES

Each person will talk about how they saw the situation and their perspective on what actually happened during the argument. The key here is not agreement on perspectives but validating one another's perspective. You will probably see the conflict differently and that's okay. Validation doesn't mean you agree with their view of things. It simply means you acknowledge their perspective and hear what they are saying. (Check out Chapter 37 on validation for more on what this should look like.)

STEP 3: IDENTIFY TRIGGERS

In conflict it's very easy to get emotionally triggered. One or both of you may have been triggered by what was said or what happened in the conflict. Our triggers are what experts call "enduring vulnerabilities" that occurred before the relationship began and have left emotional scars. If you felt triggered, try thinking back to a time in the past when you had similar feelings and share the story of what happened so your partner can better understand what triggered you during the conflict. There may have been a time when you felt judged, abandoned, powerless, bullied, out of control or unsafe and this feeling was triggered in the conflict. Share this trigger.

STEP 4: TAKE OWNERSHIP

Accept responsibility and own up to your part in the conflict. It doesn't matter if you feel like the conflict was ninety-nine percent their fault and only one percent your response. Take ownership of your one percent. Acknowledge what you did and apologize for how it contributed to the escalation of your conflict. Research has shown that taking responsibility opens up the opportunity for repair.

STEP 5: EXPLORE NEW BEHAVIORS

Now is the time to begin thinking through ways you can prevent this conflict from repeating itself in the relationship. Discuss together how you both might be able to do things differently next time. What is one way you can make it better the next time a conflict arises? What is one way your partner can make it better the next time? Create a plan to minimize hurt feelings and avoid a similar incident the next time.

The goal of moving through these five steps is not only to repair and reconnect but also to learn what triggers each of you and the patterns that keep you stuck. The military uses something called an "After Action Review" (AAR) following missions they execute to look back on what went well, what went wrong and how they can improve in the future. Our relationships deserve the same thing. This process won't be successful when emotions are high so don't attempt it during or right after a conflict. Allow some time to pass and emotions to ease before revisiting the conflict.

TAKE ACTION

Watch
How to Recover After Conflict: 5 Steps to Repairing Relationship After Conflict
on the Relationshots *YouTube* channel

We'll keep this one simple. Your "take action" activity is to pick one recent or recurrent conflict and go through the five steps together. I would suggest choosing a conflict that is not highly emotional or painful at first to get used to the process before tackling a more difficult topic.

CHAPTER 45
THE SECRET TO STAYING "IN LOVE"

I've heard countless individuals talk about how they love each other but don't feel "in love" anymore and conclude that the end of the relationship is inevitable. Their conclusion is that feelings of love and intimacy either are or are not there in relationships. It's almost as if they believe that love is some elusive emotion that comes and goes as it pleases rather than something they can actually influence and control.

Maybe you've thought or even said the words "I love you but I'm not in love with you." If so, you may be wondering whether you can fall in love again. It seems perfectly logical to me that if you once felt something for another person you can feel that once again. Of course, you can't recreate the early stage of dating where you are learning all kinds of new things about the other person and where every experience you have with them is a "first" together. It is likely, however, that you used to do some things for one another that you are no longer doing. I believe no matter where you feel like your relationship is today, you can increase your connection and fall in love again by focusing on four areas of intimacy in your relationship. Let's take a look at these four areas and how to intentionally grow in them.

RECREATIONAL INTIMACY

Recreational intimacy is simply doing things together. Sharing experiences and activities together is important to a well-balanced and healthy relationship. This is stress-free time together where you are focused on having fun and playing together. Some examples of recreational intimacy might be:
- Take a walk or work out together
- Watch a movie or play
- Attend a concert
- Play cards or a board game
- Go out for a meal or go for dessert

The goal is to enjoy each other's company free from the business of the relationship. Problem solving, resolving conflicts, discussing finances or parenting talks are off limits.

PHYSICAL INTIMACY

Physical intimacy is about both sexual and non-sexual touch. Holding hands, hugging, kissing and sexual intimacy all fulfill the human need and desire for physical touch. This is one of the areas of personal need that can only be fulfilled by your spouse, so it needs to be a priority. Sexual intimacy also happens to be one of the areas that many couples wrongly believe should just occur spontaneously with little or no intentional effort if the couple is really "in love." The key to physical intimacy is intentionality, not chemistry. If it's not occurring in the marriage you need an intentional plan for it to occur. Prioritize physical touch to increase closeness and the feelings will follow. Don't wait for the feelings to lead your actions.

EMOTIONAL INTIMACY

Emotional intimacy is the area most responsible for feeling "in love" or "out of love" with our spouse. Feeling in love is not some chemical mystery but a byproduct of intentional action. We all have certain emotional needs that lead us to feel love towards another when that person is meeting them. When those needs are not being met we conclude that we have fallen out of love.

Examples of emotional needs are admiration, affection, domestic support, honesty and openness, conversation and recreational companionship. Knowing and understanding your spouse's top emotional needs will allow you both to spend energy trying to meet these needs. When you do that regularly feelings of love will return to the relationship.

SPIRITUAL INTIMACY

Spiritual intimacy is about how you are growing in your faith as a couple. There are aspects of your faith that are personal and you grow individually through prayer, meditation, devotional time and worship. Spiritual intimacy with your spouse is about the things that you do together to grow in your relationship with God. Not only will you be growing personally but also creating deeper connection and intimacy as a couple. Examples of spiritual intimacy with your spouse might be praying together, doing a couples' devotional, attending a worship service together, talking about faith issues or serving together.

These four areas of intimacy will be the key to staying in love for a lifetime. Some of the areas may come more naturally for you than others but all four should be addressed. Don't make the mistake of allowing just one area to give you the sense of connection you desire in the relationship. An unbalanced approach will leave you feeling disconnected very quickly if something happens to prevent or reduce your interactions in that area of intimacy. Cultivate all four regularly since you and your spouse may experience the areas of intimacy differently. Spiritual intimacy may make your spouse feel most connected to you while emotional intimacy may be the area that makes you feel closest to your spouse.

TAKE ACTION

Watch
How to Fall in Love Again
on the Relationshots *YouTube* channel

1. Download the "Free Guide to Intimacy" found at **https://altaredmarriage.com.**

2. Rank yourself in each of the four areas of intimacy from 1 to 5. *(1 is needs improvement and 5 is area of strength)*

3. Identify one practical action in each area that you can do together.

4. Pull out your calendar and commit to at least one area of intimacy and one action you will do on a regular basis for the next week.

5. Evaluate how this activity together impacted the relationship and then add another area of intimacy and action for the next week. Repeat this process until you are consistently doing things in each of the four areas of intimacy.

CHAPTER 46
FORGIVING FOR REAL

Maybe you've heard the saying, "Marriage is the union of two great forgivers." It's also possible that it really isn't a common saying but there's a saying that's really similar to that. Either way, I don't think it's a stretch to say you can't maintain a healthy, long-term relationship without both giving and receiving forgiveness. You won't do everything perfectly and neither will your spouse. Forgiveness will be needed on both sides at some point. I've noticed there's a lot of confusion around what forgiveness looks like and when it should be given. There is also plenty of fear around forgiveness and wondering if it just opens the door to more of the same hurtful behavior. Complete books have been written on forgiveness so I won't be able to cover every aspect of forgiveness in this chapter. What I do want to discuss is what forgiveness is, what forgiveness is not and four steps to walking out forgiveness in your relationship.

Working with couples over the years has given me a front row seat to how people work through relational hurt, betrayal, dishonesty and infidelity. The process of forgiveness is always part of the discussion and one of the most difficult aspects of recovering and rebuilding trust. Many individuals struggle to forgive because they have a faulty view of forgiveness and wrestle with fears around forgiving their spouse and ending up in the same painful situation again down the road. I've found that a proper understanding of forgiveness helps people offer and receive forgiveness in their relationship. Let's define what forgiveness is not.

FORGIVENESS IS NOT:

1. **Minimizing:** Forgiving doesn't mean you act as if the hurt isn't a big deal.
2. **Denying:** Forgiving doesn't mean you act as if the offense never occurred.
3. **Forgetting:** Forgive and forget is a cute phrase but not a relational reality. Forgiving doesn't erase the offense.
4. **Reconciling prematurely:** Forgiving doesn't mean you rush to reconcile. There is a difference between forgiveness and reconciliation.
5. **Letting the person off the hook:** Forgiving still requires that responsibility is assigned and assumed.
6. **Being a door mat:** Forgiving doesn't mean you take the blame for another's actions or just lay down and let them treat you however they want moving forward.
7. **Taking responsibility for the other person's offense:** The offender needs to assume responsibility for their actions. Your forgiveness is not an act of taking responsibility for their offense.

FORGIVENESS IS:

1. **Dismissing a debt:** Forgiving means you choose to release the other person's debt to you.
2. **Releasing the demand that others "owe you":** Forgiving means you stop keeping a ledger of all the things the other person owes you so that you can leverage them later.
3. **Given not earned:** Forgiveness is given even if you don't believe the other person has done enough to earn it. Nobody can fully repay in a way that removes the pain and hurt.
4. **Releasing your resentment to the offender:** Even if the other person doesn't apologize or ask for forgiveness, you still release bitterness and resentment.
5. **Releasing your right to dwell on the offense:** Forgiving a debt means you choose to stop running the offense through your mind over and over.
6. **Giving up the right to bring it up all the time:** Forgiving definitely doesn't mean you forget but it does mean you choose not to remember and bring it regularly as a club to attack your spouse.

These two lists on what forgiveness is and is not are certainly not an attempt to infer that forgiveness is some easy to execute relationship principle. Forgiveness is painful, complicated and constant. You don't say, "I forgive you" one time and never have to deal with or manage that issue ever again. When the pain of a relational offense is fresh, the thought of forgiving and rebuilding trust seems impossible or a long way off. Forgiveness is a process that you commit to. As you navigate that process let me give you four steps to consider as part of the forgiveness process.

STEP 1: ACKNOWLEDGE THE OFFENSE

Name the offense. Don't dance around it, deny it or minimize it. Don't excuse the offensive behavior. Be specific about the behavior and its impact on you. You can't forgive what you don't identify: "You lied to me about where you were last night and that makes me struggle to trust your word." Be clear about what the person has done so they are faced with the decision to either accept responsibility or deny and deflect.

STEP 2: EXPERIENCE THE OFFENSE

Feel the offense. Don't deny your pain and don't deny how it has made you feel. If you care about your spouse it can be easy to empathize with any guilt or shame they may be feeling and not want to share your pain in an effort to avoid making them feel worse. Denying or ignoring your pain will not help you move forward in the forgiveness process. There will likely be a grieving process involved and it will take some time to go through all the emotions of that process. Feel every emotion you go through and be honest about how you are feeling.

STEP 3: FORGIVE THE OFFENDER

At some point you will need to make a decision to forgive your spouse for what they have done. You've already discovered what some of that forgiveness will entail from the list of what forgiveness looks like in this chapter. You will need to dismiss the debt, release what you feel is owed you and choose not to bring it up again and again. You will need to do this even if they don't seem as remorseful as you think they should be, even if they don't say "sorry like they mean it" and even if they haven't done enough to earn it. These first three steps will be a regular part of marriage because we will continually fall short and let each other down. There will be some big issues and likely lots of small issues that require our forgiveness. Master the art of these three steps so you can avoid carrying bitterness and resentment in your marriage.

STEP 4: RECONCILE IF APPROPRIATE

Forgiveness and reconciliation are not the same thing. You can forgive a person but choose not to reconcile or slow down the process of reconciliation as needed. Forgiveness can and should be offered regardless of how the other person behaves. Reconciliation requires that the offending party accept responsibility, make adjustments and commit to new behaviors and boundaries in the relationship. If you are dating and there has been a painful offense by your partner, I would recommend slowing down the progress of the relationship down quite a bit and using a "wait-and-see" approach to see if behavioral change follows verbal apologies. Let time be your friend and avoid reconciling too quickly.

If you are married then I'm clearly going to push harder for reconciliation than I would with a couple who is dating. I want to see reconciliation but I also want it to be done with wisdom. That will require community (my favorite thing) and that will require time. Healing takes time and so does change. It can be easy to want quick reconciliation so the feelings of pain and disconnection can subside and you can get back to normal again. Get others involved and allow the process to ensure true healing, growth and that change has actually occurred.

TAKE ACTION

Watch
How to Forgive: What Forgiveness Is and Is Not
on the Relationshots *YouTube* channel

1. Would you say that forgiveness is a strength or weakness for you? Why?

2. Which of the statements under "What Forgiveness Is NOT" did you associate with being a part of forgiveness? Have these beliefs prevented you from offering forgiveness in the past?

3. Which of the statements under "What Forgiveness IS" are most difficult for you to accept or practice?

4. Are there any areas of your relationship where you still believe you need to offer forgiveness? Discuss.

5. Are there any areas of your relationship where you believe you should ask your partner for forgiveness? Discuss.

6. Which of the steps to forgiveness do you struggle with, if any?

CHAPTER 47
SIX CHARACTERISTICS OF HEALTHY RELATIONSHIPS

Successful relationships are as unique and different as the individuals who make up those relationships. That's why some activities and habits work for one couple but not others. I believe every couple needs to uncover their relationship rhythm in order to enjoy a healthy and mutually satisfying marriage. They need to discover and then be intentional about making sure they are caring for each other in ways that keep them connected and allow them to manage conflict. While many characteristics of marriage are unique to each couple, there are some universal characteristics that should be present in all healthy relationships. Let's take a look at six characteristics I have observed in healthy couples.

1. LOVE

I know, deep, huh? I'm not talking about feeling "in love" here. That comes and goes. I'm talking about unconditional, sacrificial love. Check out Chapter 11: "What does it mean to love someone?" for a longer discussion on how I define love. Here is a quick overview so you don't have to mark your page and flip back right now. Love means you can feel the effects of your own behavior on your spouse. Love means you think first of making your spouse's life better. Love means you want the best for your spouse even when they can't see what it is.

2. HONESTY

"Eric is super deep." That's what you're thinking right now. Isn't it obvious that lying doesn't make for a very good relationship? Yes, that is absolutely true. Lying isn't the only component of honesty though. Many couples avoid or struggle to discuss some of the difficult areas of life and relationship. Feelings, desires, disappointments, hurts, anger, sex, failure, needs and vulnerabilities are often not shared with each other. The lack of honesty in these areas will prevent relationship growth and satisfaction.

3. FAITHFULNESS

If you are only thinking in terms of fidelity you are thinking too shallow here. A faithful spouse is one who can be trusted, depended upon and believed in. It is someone in whom you can rest securely. Faithfulness is not just a physical issue but emotional as well. A faithful spouse will guard their heart and set healthy boundaries in friendships to reserve the important and emotional conversations for their partner. Certain emotional conversations held with people outside the marriage will lead to no longer having those conversations within the relationship. (See Chapter 30 on "Should Married Couples Have Friends of the Opposite Sex?" for more on that topic.)

4. FORGIVENESS

Every relationship will require forgiveness because we all hurt each other at times. The flow of giving and receiving forgiveness in marriage will be vital to maintain connection and intimacy. Withholding forgiveness will keep you in a place of resentment, preventing the connection you desire. The previous chapter adequately covers the do's and don'ts of forgiveness so review that chapter for practical application of forgiveness in your relationship.

5. PERSONAL RESPONSIBILITY

One of the markers of emotional maturity is the ability to acknowledge how your behaviors impact others around you. A healthy relationship is one in which each person is willing to take responsibility for their emotions and behaviors. It becomes hard to feel safe and cared for when you are in relationship with someone won't take responsibility for their actions and responses. Taking personal responsibility for your emotions and behaviors helps to create a healthy atmosphere in the relationship.

6. EMPATHY

Empathy is the willingness to put yourself in your partner's shoes. It's the ability to ask yourself how they are experiencing and being impacted by the situation and then evaluating how you would feel if you were them right now. It is healthy to have the capacity to get outside of your own perspective and experience something from another person's point of view. If your spouse has ever said to you, "You're not listening to me," that's a pretty good indicator you are hearing but not empathizing with them. When you hear someone say, "They just get me," that's likely empathy at work.

Some people struggle to empathize because they don't care about a specific thing the way their spouse does. In this case, you can empathize by focusing on the emotion rather than the exact situation. You may not be able to empathize with the strength of emotions your spouse experiences when their boss gave them critical feedback about a performance because you value this type of input and don't struggle with rejection. You can, however, probably think of another situation in your life where you felt a similar feeling of failure or rejection and empathize based on those feelings, even though your spouse's current situation might not invoke those feelings for you if you were in that same situation.

I'm sure there are some other characteristics that you would add to this list of six but hopefully this provides you with a quick glimpse of some areas you can use to evaluate yourself and your relationship.

TAKE ACTION

Watch
6 Characteristics of Healthy Relationships
on the Relationshots *YouTube* channel

1. Rank yourself on a scale of 1 to 5 in each of the six characteristics: Love, Honesty, Faithfulness, Forgiveness, Personal Responsibility and Empathy. *(1 being area of strength and 5 being an area of growth)*

2. Which of the six characteristics do you believe needs some growth in your life?

3. Tell your spouse which of the six characteristics you see as a strength of theirs. Explain why.

4. What is one thing you will commit to this week to grow in the area you identified in question 2?

CHAPTER 48
THE #1 RELATIONSHIP KILLER

If we're honest with ourselves, we probably do a lot of things that cause our relationships to struggle but I've noticed one thing that rises to the top of my list of relationship killers. For most of us this skill comes naturally and often unconsciously. A lot of times we don't even notice we're doing it. The number one relationship killer is criticism. Before you start rolling your eyes thinking I'm suggesting you can't ever share a concern you have with your spouse, let me explain.

There is a big difference between a complaint and a criticism. A complaint is focused on a specific issue while a criticism is an attack of the person. A complaint sounds like this. "Could you please make sure to pick up your clothes after you shower and not leave them on the bathroom floor for me to pick up?" A criticism sounds like this. "I'm tired of you always leaving your clothes all over the place. You're so selfish and don't think of anyone but yourself."

Leading experts in the field of psychology and relationships all agree that criticism is one of the most devastating behaviors in a relationship. Drs. John and Julie Gottman identify criticism as one of their four horseman that inevitably lead to divorce. Sue Johnson, the founder of Emotion-Focused Therapy, sees criticism as a key issue that keeps couples disconnected and stuck in negative cycles. Couples need to cultivate a safe place where they feel secure and known in order to fight against remaining in a defensive posture in the relationship. When criticism occurs regularly in a relationship it tends to have the following effects.

1. CRITICISM DIMINISHES SELF-ESTEEM

The childhood rhyme about how "sticks and stones may break bones but words will never hurt" is a lie. Words cut deep. Criticism hurts and impacts how we view ourselves. It can make a person question their value and worth. Enough criticism and a person can start to believe they are what their criticizer says they are.

2. CRITICISM ERODES TRUST

Consistent criticism can feel like betrayal. It violates the belief that the person you love will care how you feel and not hurt you. Criticism can make you question whether your spouse will be there for you when you need them. It becomes difficult to trust someone that you don't feel safe being yourself around.

3. CRITICISM DESTROYS INTIMACY

Has your spouse ever criticized you and then tried to initiate sex a few hours later? If so, how did that work for them? I'm guessing the response was less than warm and welcoming. Criticism creates emotional distance between you and your partner. Vulnerability and trust are necessary for true intimacy and criticism fights against both of these.

4. CRITICISM TRIGGERS DEFENSIVENESS

You may have discovered that criticism actually moves a person more towards their position than it does bring them closer to your perspective. I know many individuals who desire change in their spouse and believe criticism to be a good technique to influence this change. It rarely works to cause the desired change and usually just pushes the person further away. Criticism causes a person to dig in their heels, resisting change and hurts the connection in the process. That's why the chapters on validation and appreciation (Chapters 37 and 42) are so important to set a positive atmosphere before trying to give critical feedback in a relationship.

If we understand the underlying emotion that often drives our criticism in the relationship, we will be able to better communicate our desires, while avoiding critical statements. It may be that you desire connection and closeness with your spouse but they always seem to be too busy to connect. Instead of expressing your desires it can be easy to just criticize your spouse for being unavailable, absent or selfish rather than asking when they could be available to have undistracted time with you. If you have a tendency to criticize, pause and think about what you really desire and ask for that instead.

Personality differences are another area that trip couples up with criticism. Your spouse may be someone who likes to process information and asks questions of you to stay connected in the relationship. Those who desire information ask questions to become informed but can come across to their partners as being critical. The questions can make the other person feel like their spouse doesn't trust them, doesn't think they are competent or is second-guessing their decisions. Questions that were intended to be informational now come across as critical. If your spouse's questions feel like criticism to you, express that and seek to move towards each other in this area. They can commit to asking fewer questions and you can commit to believing their questions are for information and not meant to be critical of you.

Whether criticism in the relationship is unconscious, unintentional or used as a manipulative control tactic, you can count on it damaging the relationship. You must learn to complain without criticism and address specific concerns without conveying judgment or condemnation if you hope to maintain connection and avoid damaging your relationship. Criticism will kill connection.

TAKE ACTION

Watch
#1 Relationship Killer
on the Relationshots *YouTube* channel

1. Do you like to ask your spouse questions to gain information and connect? If so, ask them if these questions feel like criticism to them.

2. Do you have a tendency to use criticism in an attempt to influence your spouse? If so, what is it that you really desire?

3. Which of the four effects of criticism listed have you experienced in your relationship?

4. Are there things your spouse says or does that feel like criticism to you? Give some specific examples.

5. How would you like your spouse to approach you with issues or concerns they may have so you don't feel criticized?

6. What is one thing you will commit to this week to avoid criticizing your spouse?

CHAPTER 49
TIPS FOR HANDLING DIFFICULT CONVERSATIONS

One of the keys to a healthy relationship is the way a couple handles difficult conversations. In nearly three decades of marriage, my wife and I have had a good number of difficult conversations and I can honestly say that I've handled a lot of them poorly. My emotions get involved, my pride gets in the way, my insecurities get exposed and the conversation often goes sideways. Maybe you can relate. I've discovered that the key to handling difficult conversations well is not just what you do and say during the conversation but also how you approach the discussion. When approaching a difficult conversation in your relationship, consider the following eight tips.

1. PRAY

If you are a person of faith, prayer should be your starting point for any difficult conversation. Check your heart. Look in the mirror and examine yourself before approaching your partner. Ask God for wisdom in the conversation you are about to start.

2. BE CLEAR ABOUT THE ISSUE

When preparing for a difficult conversation you need to ask yourself a few clarifying questions. What is the specific behavior or issue that is causing the problem? What is the impact this behavior or issue is having on you? You need to be clear so you can articulate the issue in two to three statements, avoiding tangents and confusion. You can't manage a difficult conversation well if you bounce all over the place, bringing up multiple different things.

3. KNOW YOUR OBJECTIVE

What do you want to accomplish? What is your desired outcome? Do you have a goal other than just "making sure they get a piece of your mind?" When the conversation concludes, what would you like to happen? Is there something you would like the other person to do and how will you support that decision? Has an agreement been reached? If you don't have a desired outcome you won't be able to judge the success of the conversation.

4. HAVE A LEARNING MINDSET

You should approach a difficult conversation with a desire to learn and understand your spouse better. You are likely starting the discussion to address an issue but don't assume you already know your partner's perspectives, beliefs or motives around the issue. Be open to learning and listening. This will require you to ask more than tell. Be more inquisitive and less declarative.

5. MANAGE YOUR EMOTIONS

Emotional decisions and statements are rarely accurate. Emotions distort reality. Feelings skew the facts. Nobody recalls past conflict and conversations perfectly because our emotions get involved and influence how we remember. You will need to manage your emotions before you show up for the conversation and throughout the difficult discussion. When your emotions begin to take over your partner will likely respond with defensiveness. If your emotions start escalating, take a break to cool off and then come back to the conversation another time.

You may have noticed that these first five tips occur before you have even started the conversation. As I mentioned in the opening paragraph, your approach to a difficult conversation is as important as what happens during the conversation.

6. CHOOSE THE RIGHT TIME AND PLACE TO HAVE THE CONVERSATION

It's possible to ruin your chances of having a good conversation simply by failing to find a good place and time to begin. Don't do it when either of you is tired. Don't try to squeeze it in quick leaving little or no time for dialogue. Don't do it in front of other people. It's best to ask your spouse when it would be a good time for them to have a discussion.

7. KNOW HOW TO BEGIN

Nobody appreciates the old conversation ambush where you invite the other person to lunch and then ambush them with the real issue you wanted to discuss. Be up front and direct with your intentions. "Hey babe, I want to discuss your spending. Can we talk about this tonight after dinner?" When you actually do begin the conversation, psychologist John Gottman recommends the "soft startup." Avoid negative emotions and bring a legitimate complaint rather than blaming or criticizing. This will increase your chances of getting a positive response in return.

8. PRIORITIZE THE RELATIONSHIP

The goal of difficult conversations is to strengthen the relationship, not destroy it. When addressing a sensitive issue, you must remain focused on the long term health of the relationship rather than on getting your way or being right. Too many couples get so narrowly focused on the present issue they lose sight of the bigger picture. Avoid statements that will cut deep and hurt your partner. Be careful of comments you can't take back. If you don't find full resolution in this moment there will be more opportunities in the future to try again. If the conversation starts going poorly you can end it and revisit the issue later.

Difficult conversations are both inevitable and necessary when cultivating a strong, healthy relationship. These eight tips won't guarantee success but will definitely set you up for a better chance at navigating conversations that have the potential to become personal, emotional and escalate.

TAKE ACTION

Watch
8 Tips for Handling Difficult Conversations
on the Relationshots *YouTube* channel

1. Do you tend to step into difficult conversations or avoid them? Why?

2. Are there dynamics in your relationship that make you fearful to have a difficult conversation? If so, what are they?

3. Do you consider yourself to be a safe place for your spouse? Does your spouse agree?

4. Which of the eight tips do you need to work on the most?

5. If there is a difficult conversation that you believe needs to take place in your relationship, apply tips six and seven right now. Tell your spouse the specific issue you would like to address and then set a day and time to have the conversation. (If you have implemented the staff meeting suggestion from Chapter 39 you may already have a specific time).

CHAPTER 50
HOW TO REBUILD TRUST AFTER LYING

Trust is a tricky thing in relationships. It's not only impacted by what has occurred in your current relationship but also by trust baggage you bring with you from past relationships. Trust is one of those things that takes a lifetime to build yet can be destroyed in a moment. Because trust is necessary for a healthy relationship and because we all fall short at times, learning how to rebuild trust becomes a key skill for maintaining relationships.

Rebuilding trust after one instance of dishonesty is much easier than doing so when your partner has a repeated pattern of deception. In fact, if you are still in the dating process and your partner has a pattern of dishonesty I would strongly encourage you to pause or end the relationship. This character issue will not just disappear one day when they "grow up", especially if it has been a pervasive pattern in their life. If you are married and your spouse has a pattern of dishonesty, I would recommend you seek counseling to help get to the root of the issue and to set healthy boundaries in that process of discovery and healing. If your relationship has been damaged by deception and you need to rebuild trust with your spouse for instances of dishonesty tied to a specific issue or short season of time, consider these five keys for rebuilding trust.

1. TAKE FULL ACCOUNTABILITY

Don't blame your partner or outside circumstances. It can be easy to look for "reasons why" you have lied in order to excuse or justify the behavior. It may be that your partner doesn't create an environment where you are rewarded for honesty but instead are made to pay if they don't like what you are doing or sharing. Even if your spouse doesn't provide a safe space for you to share and this is an issue that needs to be addressed in the relationship, you still need to take full responsibility for choosing to lie. You can discuss the things you would like to see changed in the relationship at another time but initially you to need to fully own your lies. Failure to do so will make it hard for your partner to believe they can trust you again.

2. EVALUATE YOURSELF

Do you know why you choose to lie? If your spouse has a tendency to lie you are probably answering this question out loud right now. "Yeah, I know why they lie. It's because they're a dirty liar!" People lie for a reason and not all lies have the same motive. Some people lie to look good or brag. Some lie to avoid conflict. Some lie for acceptance and approval. Some lie for fear of losing closeness in the relationship. Some people lie because they are selfish or evil.

If you struggle with lying you need to address the deeper issues and work on yourself. If you lie to avoid conflict then you need to get more comfortable with healthy conflict. If you lie for acceptance then maybe you need to work on self-esteem. If you lie for fear of losing love or closeness in the relationship then you might need to address some co-dependency issues. You must understand why you do something if you hope to change those beliefs and behaviors in the future.

3. COMMIT TO UNWAVERING HONESTY

When you are rebuilding trust in a relationship you have to avoid little lies or oversights at all costs. There is no room in the trust rebuilding process for even small "omissions" of information. Trust is not simply the avoidance of deception but also a commitment to over communicate. Don't allow gaps in information so your partner has to fill those in. In the absence of information they will create their own narrative about what is going on and that will be tied to you being dishonest. When trust has been broken your spouse will not assume the best or give you the benefit of the doubt.

4. BE PATIENT

Rebuilding trust takes time. Your spouse will need to process and heal from the dishonesty. It will take time to trust and believe again. You may be remorseful and fully committed to being open and honest moving forward but they can't see your heart or intentions. Your spouse can only evaluate based on your actions and that will take time. Avoid the tendency to pressure your partner to hurry up and trust again. Patience will show that you both empathize with their hurt and value their experience.

5. BE CONSISTENT

As with most things in relationship and life, consistency is king. You can talk a good game and say all the right things. You can even modify your behavior over the short-term but long-term consistency will be the key to rebuilding trust. Inconsistency makes it hard for others to trust you.

Some people suggest that trust is like a vase that once broken can be glued back together but will never be the same. I disagree. If you have a good understanding of why the dishonesty occurred and pursue personal healing and consistency in new patterns and behaviors, trust can be fully restored. The greater depth and intentionality in communication required for the trust building process will also produce a more connected and communicative relationship in the long run. Be willing to do the work to rebuild what you have broken and the relationship can be made whole again.

TAKE ACTION

Watch
How to Rebuild Trust After Lying in a Relationship
on the Relationshots *YouTube* channel

1. Has trust been broken in your relationship due to dishonesty? If so, what are some of those instances?

2. If trust has been broken, what has been done to rebuild trust? What else needs to occur?

3. If you struggle to trust your spouse at times, what can they do to help rebuild trust with you?

4. Would you describe your spouse as a "safe place" to talk about anything and everything? If so, why? If not, why not?

5. If dishonesty is not an issue in your relationship, are there any areas where better or more consistent communication would help to build transparency and greater connection for you? What are those areas?

6. What will you both commit to in moving forward to rebuild trust or build greater trust and intimacy in your relationship?

CHAPTER 51
HOW TO MAINTAIN HEALTHY SEX IN MARRIAGE

Sexual intimacy is one of the main areas in marriage where couples struggle to get on the same page. Whether it's mismatched sex drives, different beliefs about sex or past sexual trauma and abuse, it can be difficult to maintain a healthy and mutually satisfying sexual relationship in marriage. When you add to those complexities the vulnerability needed to have healthy sexual intimacy, you have a recipe for guilt, shame and defensiveness when sex is brought up by one spouse.

Not only is sex difficult to talk about without one or both of you feeling attacked but sexual intimacy also seems to be impacted by anything and everything in the relationship. Maybe you've noticed a few of the following things getting in the way of your sex life: children, work, busy schedules, fatigue, headaches, hormonal changes, disconnection, lack of emotional intimacy, poor body image, performance anxiety, hygiene, a disappointing ending to your favorite TV show, warring countries on the other side of the world and on and on and on. Some of those may be exaggerations but you get the idea. Things get in the way of sex.

If you're struggling to create and maintain a healthy sexual relationship in your marriage, this chapter won't single-handedly resolve your issues but can definitely get you moving in the right direction. If sexual trauma or abuse are negatively impacting your intimacy, I would suggest you seek a licensed counselor who specializes in sex, as the impact of that trauma is complex and far reaching. There is definitely hope for you to heal and build a satisfying sexual relationship but you'll likely need some outside help. For many couples, the following four keys can be helpful in getting you unstuck and on the road to great sex in your marriage.

1. DEAL WITH THE PAST

As I just mentioned, you may need some professional assistance in this area of your relationship if you have experienced abuse, rape or sexual assault. One of the reasons many couples struggle sexually is because they bring past baggage from unhealthy relationships, faulty mindsets and models about sex and guilt or shame around previous experiences. All of these will play into how you view or handle sex in your marriage; you can't ignore the past if it is negatively impacting your present relationship. Talk about your past, pursue healing and seek outside help when necessary.

2. PURSUE PURITY

Sexual intimacy for many couples is unconsciously driven by the impurity of one or both spouses. Many individuals have a high desire and drive for sex because they regularly feed their minds with sexual food. Viewing porn, scrolling through pictures on social media and watching movies with high sexual content will create a hunger in your flesh for the sex you have been feeding yourself visually. You then turn to your spouse with this appetite and expect them to satisfy the hunger you've created from your own immorality.

Filling your mind with erotic images and entering the bedroom with unhealthy or unrealistic expectations based on some fictitious scenario crafted by adult performers will negatively impact your sexual intimacy in the marriage. One aspect of protecting the sexual relationship with your spouse is guarding your eyes and mind outside of the bedroom.

3. COMMUNICATE OFTEN ABOUT SEX

Very few couples communicate well about their sexual relationship. Some even have a satisfying sex life yet don't talk about it while others don't have a mutually satisfying sex life and struggle to talk about it. Sex in marriage is not a "once solved always solved" situation. Every stage of life and marriage will bring about different challenges to the sexual relationship. Your calendar, children, hormones, careers and self-image issues will change the sexual dynamic throughout the life of your marriage. What works for you both sexually in one season will likely not work in another season.

Your sexual intimacy needs to be an area of the relationship that you discuss regularly, especially when one or both of you is not feeling fully connected or satisfied in this area. Normalize talking about this part of your marriage as this will be necessary to maintain connection sexually. Don't buy into the lie that sex should always be good if your relationship is good and you shouldn't have to discuss it or work at it. That's simply not true. If you already have a regular staff meeting each week (Chapter 39: The Business of Marriage), then sexual intimacy could be a regular discussion topic to cover so you don't just bring it up when things are not going well. Get used to asking each other how you're feeling about your sexual intimacy even when it's good.

4. PRIORITIZE IT

If sex isn't occurring to your satisfaction in the relationship, don't wait around hoping it will correct itself. Like anything else in your relationship, if it is important for your marriage but isn't happening regularly, schedule it. Scheduling sex doesn't mean something is wrong, it means you value it enough to make sure it happens when life seems to be getting in the way. Scheduling sex also doesn't make it less enjoyable. If you have a favorite restaurant, I'm guessing that knowing you have a 7:00pm reservation this Friday doesn't somehow make your favorite food taste bad when you get there. On the contrary, the reservation actually builds anticipation as you look forward to something you know you will enjoy. Why should sex be any different?

If you want to check out an entire video on scheduled sex, head over to the Relationshots Youtube channel and search for "Does Scheduled Sex Actually Work?" Scheduling sex does three things for your sexual intimacy. First, it prioritizes this important aspect of your marriage. Planning ensures that you aren't leaving your intimacy to chance. Second, it eliminates sexual rejection. Many couples stop initiating sex because they have been rejected in the past and don't want to experience that again so they just stop initiating. Knowing what day and time you have set aside for sex eliminates the possibility that one will initiate and the other turn them down. Lastly, scheduled sex produces spontaneous sex. The majority of couples I know who schedule sex find that it also leads to other times of spontaneous sex. Scheduled sex doesn't mean you can't have sex other times as well. It simply means you want to make sure you aren't drifting into a sexless marriage.

Make discussions about sex a normal part of your communication rhythm in the marriage. Anything you want to be successful in your relationship will require that you talk about it, prioritize it and protect it. Sex is no different.

TAKE ACTION

Watch
How to Maintain Healthy Sex in Marriage
on the Relationshots *YouTube* channel

1. How would you rate your current sexual intimacy in the marriage from 1 to 5? *(1 being ice cold and 5 being red hot)*

2. How often would you each like to be having sex each week in your marriage?

3. How often do you currently talk about your sexual relationship? If you don't discuss it very often or ever, why not?

4. Are there any purity issues that need to be addressed that are negatively impacting your sexual intimacy? *(unhealthy expectations, comparison, unwanted pressure from spouse, etc.)*

5. If you have been struggling to stay consistent with your sexual intimacy, would you be open to scheduling sex?

6. What are you going to commit to this week to create or maintain a healthy sex life? *(schedule it, talk more about it, pursue purity)*

CHAPTER 52
SUCCESSFUL COUPLES DO THIS ONE THING

What if I told you that one, super simple, not so obvious interaction in a relationship had great power in determining if couples divorced or stayed together? What if I told you it might be occurring in your relationship right now and you are missing it and missing a great opportunity to ensure the success of your relationship? We often make marriage more difficult than it needs to be, focusing on trying to resolve some of the unresolvable issues (Chapter 33) while missing out on regular opportunities to connect and grow closer to one another.

Research done following newlywed couples, discovered that after six years of marriage the couples who had divorced did something simple only 33% of the time while the couples who remained married did this same thing 86% of the time. That's a huge difference and worth taking note of. And if you're still with me, I'm guessing you want to know what that one thing is. Researcher and psychologist John Gottman calls it "turning towards." There are only two postures in a relationship, you are either turning towards or turning away from your marriage. You are either "leaning into" or "leaning away" from your partner. There is no such thing as neutral in relationship. A relationship is either growing or decreasing in connection.

If you want to grow in your relationship, leaning towards your spouse when they attempt to connect with you becomes key. On any given day, both you and your spouse will make "bids" looking for a response. When a bid is made the other person will choose to either lean into that bid or lean away from the bid. Practically, here's what that might look like. You are sitting on the couch watching TV or reading a book and your spouse looks out the window and says, "It's a beautiful day today." That is a bid. You can turn towards them and respond to their bid with something positive like, "It is. We should go for a walk." Even a response as simple as "yep" counts as leaning in. You can also choose to ignore them or argue with them about the weather which would be leaning away from them.

It is easy to miss bids if you aren't looking for them because they may be subtle and so common you have begun to ignore them. Your wife is sitting on the couch across the room from you and begins to laugh at something on her phone. This might be a bid to connect, hoping you will ask what is funny. Your husband is in bed reading a book and says out loud, "That's a great idea." This may be a bid for you to ask what he just read. When a bid occurs, healthy couples recognize and respond to those bids the majority of the time. There are many different types of bids to watch for in your relationship. Following are seven common bids to be aware of and watch for in your marriage. [8]

1. PAY ATTENTION

"How does this look?" "Did you just see that?"

2. SIMPLE REQUEST

"Can you grab me a drink while you're up?" "Can you take out the trash?"

3. HELP ME

"Let's go get some decorations for the party." "Will you return these clothes when you go to the mall?"

---

[8] Zach Brittle, "Turning Towards Instead of Away," Gottman.com, Gottman Institute, 2022, https://www.gottman.com/blog/turn-toward-instead-of-away/.

4. CHAT WITH ME

"You'll never guess what happened at work today?" "Did you hear about the flooding in Missouri?"

5. SHARE WITH ME

"How was your day?" "Did you have fun with your friends tonight?"

6. BE AFFECTIONATE

"Come cuddle with me on the couch." "You look like you need a hug." Any touch or embrace without saying anything.

7. JOIN ME

"Let's take a cooking class together." "Would you ever want to take a dance lesson?"

When you begin to watch for bids from your spouse, you will see multiple opportunities each day to respond and lean towards the relationship. If you don't believe your spouse makes bids for connection, it could be they have stopped doing so because they learned over time that you weren't likely to lean into those bids. None of us likes rejection so if we don't feel like our partner is responding to our bids we will stop making them to avoid the feelings of rejection. If you have both stopped making bids, I encourage you to have a conversation about this and commit to initiating bids again.

TAKE ACTION

Watch
Successful Couples Do This One Thing
on the Relationshots *YouTube* channel

1. On a scale of 1 to 5 how would you rate yourself in making bids for connection? *(1 being never and 5 being often)*

2. Do you feel like your spouse responds positively and regularly to your bids for connection? Why or why not? Give some examples.

3. If you don't feel like your spouse "leans into" your bids, how does that make you feel?

4. Which of the seven bids listed in this chapter do you make most often? What is your goal in making this bid? *(learning, feeling heard or seen, physical touch, emotional connection, etc.)*

5. Commit this week to both making bids and responding to your spouse's bids. After the week is over, evaluate how you both did and the impact that had on your relationship.

Epilogue

You did it! I'm assuming you didn't flip straight to the end of the book but you've actually worked your way through many or all of the chapters and intentionally applied the relevant concepts to your relationship. If so, congratulations! Not just for completing the book and for being intentional in your relationship but for the growth I know you've experienced. You can't put regular effort into your relationship and not see the results. Good results are a natural byproduct of intentional effort.

I began this book by giving you my philosophy of marriage, weeding and feeding. In the first chapter I laid out what I believe to be the three essential keys to successful marriages: Intentionality, Personal Responsibility and Community. My hope is that you saw and experienced the importance of these three areas woven throughout every chapter and concept covered. I really do believe relationships are quite simple. They're not easy because people are emotional and complicated but the components of a healthy relationship really aren't all that complicated.

INTENTIONALITY

Regularly do the little and big things in your relationship that allow you both to feel connected and cared for. Create a rhythm for your day, week, month and year that prioritizes your relationship and the key moments and conversations needed. Don't leave anything you believe to be important for your relationship up to chance. Nobody stumbles into a great relationship. If needed, schedule date nights, times of communication, sex, budget talks and connection moments.

PERSONAL RESPONSIBILITY

Relationships are only as strong as the health of the two individuals involved. If you want a strong marriage you need to be fully committed to your own personal growth and healing. Many couples spend more energy complaining about and trying to get their partner to change than they do on personal improvement. Personal growth is a lifelong journey not a one-time action. Different seasons of your marriage will expose different areas of needed growth in both of your lives. You may have found healing and growth in your life in one season, only to find a different season requires additional growth. I was forced to grow in patience and selflessness early in my marriage only to find the addition of children required a whole new level of growth in these areas. Your marriage commitment requires you to grow as much personally as you will relationally with your spouse.

COMMUNITY

Hopefully you didn't get tired of me talking about community throughout the book. If you skipped Chapter 36, shame on you! I really do believe community is the most important thing for successful marriages. We were not meant to take the marriage journey alone. Our community will provide support and security for our relationships in those difficult seasons when we feel like giving up and can't see a future where things are different. Healthy couples are committed to connecting with others regularly in community. If you don't have an authentic community of couples who will support you, talk about the realities and struggles of relationship and encourage you to keep going when you don't have the strength to do so, we invite you to join us. The Altared Marriage Membership community was created for couples just like you. We know your struggle. We share our struggles. We support one another. We're intentional about growing our marriages together. We would love to walk with you on your relationship journey.

Visit **https://altaredmarriage.com/membership** to learn more and connect with real couples committed to their relationships.

I believe every couple has the ability to build a healthy, mutually satisfying marriage that goes the distance. No matter how you started or how it's been going, your future marriage is still before you. You get to determine what it looks like. You are in control of the effort you put into your relationship. You may need some outside help to get unstuck or some new skills or tools that will help you succeed in your relationship but I believe you have what it takes. Find your community, establish an intentional rhythm for growth and connection and you can create the marriage you've always dreamed. I believe in you and I'm committed to helping you experience a healthy, thriving marriage.

For additional resources visit
www.altaredmarriage.com

Acknowledgments

I am grateful to so many people for their assistance in the creation of this book and their contributions to my life personally. First, to my wife, Jill. You can't write a book about relationships without first acknowledging the primary place you both learn about relationship and the parts of yourself you'd rather ignore. Without experiencing the highs and lows of my own marriage I would never have developed the passion and skills to help others strengthen their relationships. I'm grateful for the moments of fun and laughter, the difficult moments that forced me to practice what I preach and even the painful times our relationship has exposed the parts of myself I wish didn't exist. I'm better for taking this journey of marriage with you and wouldn't be who I am without you.

I am grateful for the example of marriage modeled by my parents, Willy and Joan Wooten. You have loved each other well and demonstrated healthy marriage commitment for me and countless others during your fifty years of marriage and counting. You have supported my marriage and mission in ways no one else will ever know. I wouldn't still be on this journey without your prayers, encouragement and financial support. You are both in the pages of this book. Especially you, Joan, with your grammatical and punctuation critiques!

I am grateful for the team of people who believe in me enough to sacrifice their time, effort and skills in making this book a reality. Donella, thank you for the hours spent reading, crossing out my overuse of commas and helping to make this book better and me appear more competent. Randi, thank you for pushing me, supporting me and making this book a reality. This book would continue to be a "project for later" if you didn't look me in the eye and ask, "When is the earliest you can finish this book?" Thank you for always making time to meet and then promptly emailing me the list of things I committed to or you committed me to do!

I am grateful for my community, the group of people I refer to as the Marriage Mafia. Marriage truly is "family business." Thank you to all the couples who have supported my marriage, challenged my faulty beliefs and held me accountable to live out the covenant commitment I made to my marriage. Thank you to all the couples who see value in being a part of the Altared Marriage Membership community. Thank you to all the couples who have joined me in counseling, attended marriage classes, travelled to other countries for an Altared Marriage Experience and trusted me to partner with you on your relationship journey. Your stories, your intentionality, your highs and lows and your wisdom have inspired my marriage and shaped my approach to helping couples.

I am grateful to Danni White and the team at DW Creative Publishers for your guidance in making this book a reality. Your graciousness, professionalism and wisdom were invaluable to me on this publishing journey.

Topical Index

COMMUNICATION

Chapter 15: Five Communication Killers in a Relationship
Chapter 34: Five Mistakes We Make When Listening
Chapter 37: The Importance of Validation
Chapter 41: Why Couples Stop Sharing With Each Other
Chapter 48: The #1 Relationship Killer
Chapter 49: Tips for Handling Difficult Conversations

CONFLICT

Chapter 3: The #1 Mistake Couples Make in Conflict
Chapter 14: Four Keys to Resolving Conflict
Chapter 19: Managing Differences
Chapter 23: "Managing the Moment"
Chapter 24: How to Compromise
Chapter 31: The 3 Sides of Conflict
Chapter 33: Resolvable Issues and Perpetual Problems
Chapter 44: Five Steps to Repairing After Conflict
Chapter 46: Forgiving for Real

CONNECTION

Chapter 4: Two Tips to Increase Emotional Connection
Chapter 12: Three Things Husbands Want From Their Wives
Chapter 13: Three Things Wives Want From Their Husbands
Chapter 22: Three Questions to Emotionally Connect With Your Spouse
Chapter 32: Three Keys to Emotional Safety
Chapter 38: Three Connection Killers
Chapter 42: The Power of Appreciation
Chapter 45: The Secret to Staying "In Love"
Chapter 52: Successful Couples Do This One Thing

ATTACHMENT & TRUST

Chapter 5: Understanding Your Attachment Style

Chapter 17: Enemies of Trust in a Relationship

Chapter 27: Seven Triggers for Those With Avoidant Attachment Style

Chapter 28: Seven Triggers for Those With Avoidant Attachment Style

Chapter 50: How to Rebuild Trust After Lying

SEXUAL INTIMACY

Chapter 8: Five Things That Hinder Sex in a Relationship

Chapter 43: What's Acceptable Sexually in Marriage

Chapter 51: What's Acceptable Sexually in Marriage

BOUNDARIES

Chapter 6: Boundaries in Relationship

Chapter 20: Three Levels of Boundaries

LOGISTICS

Chapter 39: The Business of Marriage

Chapter 40: Five Reasons to Combine Your Finances

Chapter 16: Is Your Baggage Impacting Your Relationship?

www.ingramcontent.com/pod-product-compliance
Lightning Source LLC
Chambersburg PA
CBHW072000110526
44592CB00012B/1152